SIMONE
WEIL

Edited and with an introduction by ERIC O. SPRINGSTED

SIMONE WEIL

Late Philosophical Writings

Translated by ERIC O. SPRINGSTED *and* LAWRENCE E. SCHMIDT

University of Notre Dame Press
Notre Dame, Indiana

University of Notre Dame Press
Notre Dame, Indiana 46556
www.undpress.nd.edu

Library of Congress Cataloging-in-Publication Data

Weil, Simone, 1909–1943.
[Works. Selections. English. 2015]
Late philosophical writings / Simone Weil ;
edited and with an introduction by Eric O. Springsted ;
translated by Eric O. Springsted and Lawrence E. Schmidt.
pages   cm
Includes bibliographical references and index.
ISBN 978-0-268-04150-2 (pbk. : alk. paper)
ISBN 0-268-04150-4 (pbk. : alk. paper)
I. Springsted, Eric O., editor.   II. Title.
B2430.W472E55   2015
194—dc23
2015017676

Contents

Notes on the Texts and Acknowledgments

With the exception of "What Is Sacred in Every Human Being?," which comes from the time Weil was in London in 1943, all of the texts presented here were written during her time in Marseille — September 1940 to May 1942. The texts used are the ones established and published in the *Oeuvres complètes* IV.1 and IV.2 (Paris: Gallimard, 2008, 2009), again excepting "What Is Sacred in Every Human Being?," which comes from *Écrits de Londres* (Paris: Gallimard, 1957). In the case of three essays, the *Oeuvres complètes* edition varies from earlier editions, most notably in a number of additional pages included in "At the Price of an Infinite Error: The Scientific Image, Ancient and Modern," the arrangement of various paragraphs in "God in Plato," and some small changes in "The First Condition for the Work of a Free Person," where Weil's original is restored after certain editorial changes had been made by the publication for which that essay was intended. This is the first English edition of these essays in their complete and corrected form.

Three essays are also translated and published in book form in English for the first time here: "Essay on the Concept of Reading," "Some Reflections on the Concept of Value," and "Notes on the Concept of Character."

Titles in some cases have been changed from their first English translation. "Human Personality" is here "What Is Sacred in Every Human Being?"; "Morality and Literature" is "Literature and Morals"; "The Responsibility of Writers" is "The Responsibilities of Literature"; "The First Condition of Non-Servile Work" is "The First Condition for the Work of a Free Person"; "Classical Science and After" is "At the Price of an Infinite Error: The Scientific Image, Ancient and Modern."

The translation of "Some Reflections on the Concept of Value" was originally published in *Philosophical Investigations* 37.2 (2014): 105–12, and is reprinted by permission of Wiley-Blackwell.

I would like to thank Lawrence Schmidt for his kind and gracious offer to include his translation of "The First Condition for the Work of a Free Person." I would also like to thank my longtime friend and philosophical correspondent, Stephen Goldman, for his reading of several of these translations, his suggestions, and above all for the conversation that followed.

Introduction

Simone Weil on Philosophy

It can be highly misleading to separate out a complex thinker's works too neatly into discrete subjects if one wants to understand the thinker herself. This is especially the case with somebody such as Simone Weil. Her works cover philosophy, history, social matters (such as justice, labor, and politics), mysticism, world religions, and subjects belonging to Christian theology. Valuable as these insights may be to those fields individually, there is an intellectual character to all of them that clearly shows they come from a single, and singular, mind. The insights are valuable in themselves, but the thinker transcends them. For anyone to say who Weil is as a thinker, and what she has to teach anybody, and to say it accurately, much less well, one ultimately has to take into consideration all of her work as a whole and its complex overlapping.

Still, it can be a very helpful exercise to take up the question of Weil's thinking about philosophy as a particular subject, that is, to take up what she thought thinking is and ought to be and hence what she thought she was doing in writing all that she did. It is to take up what she thought the value of her work was and, as it turns out, what her thinking on value was.

But in treating what Weil thought philosophy is, we need to be careful about what exactly we are doing. Numerous books and articles on Weil have treated her from a philosophical point of view. But doing so can present certain problems, most generally when one fails to see where her interests and concerns go far beyond what academic philosophers normally treat. There are a number of places where this happens. Above all, to approach her in a strictly philosophical way will often completely miss—often deliberately—a genuine and central theological commitment in Simone Weil the thinker, or will miss it *as* a theological or religious commitment. Her Christianity, as unorthodox as it often appears, is not an addendum or a conclusion to a chain of reasoning from elsewhere. For her, there really is an act of God that takes place in Christ's Incarnation and Crucifixion that determines the nature of the world and of human beings. This conviction was something she herself admits that she came by unexpectedly through personal experience, and not by a process of reasoning. She even goes so far as to suggest that her reason wasn't quite sure what to do with what was indeed a certitude in her life. Yet, lest one mistake things on the other side, it also needs to be understood that this religious commitment does not make serious and unremitting philosophical reflection beside the point for Weil. Far from it. She is not just an anthology of mystical insights. So, how this commitment *and* philosophy go together is of the first order for understanding Weil. It is a matter of getting it right on both sides of the equation.

A second mistake occurs when one treats her as a philosopher in the sense that she is somebody who produces a philosophy. This is more than a problem of ignoring the obvious and oft-repeated fact that Weil is not a systematic thinker. Even though she is not, she is not an incoherent thinker, and what she says in one place often really does have bearing on what she says elsewhere. She thinks in a highly analogical way and finds some very startling and striking connections between otherwise disparate areas of thought. For this reason, it really is possible to provide some sort of conceptual map of the distinctive parts of her thinking. It is possible to teach somebody what significant things she has to say, and it is possible to show a person how to move from one concept to another in her thought. She is not an oracle. Rather, the mistake comes in thinking that once one has provided such a map that one has said what she was trying to do as a philosopher. For example, one might be tempted once such a map has been drawn then to compare her various "positions" as a philosopher with those of other philosophers. Though she has startling and discernible positions, one might be tempted to think that such positions are what she thinks philosophers ought to be coming up with, and that philosophy, as it is in the academy, is a matter of continually arguing for and against these positions. One can see where this has happened in treating Weil, even from the very beginning of the secondary literature on her. For example, Miklos Vetö, in his early and still very helpful *The Religious Metaphysics of Simone Weil*, provides a way to navigate around Weil's thinking that is quite accurate and insightful.[1] He is also quite helpful in regularly pointing out the degree to which Weil was indebted to Plato and to Kant. But Vetö also was insistent that Weil was a "classical metaphysician," which is to say, he thinks that she was doing something like building a position, and that not only can one compare it to others, say, Kant, but that one intellectually ought to be doing that. But that is exactly what is at stake, at least insofar as Weil herself saw the nature of philosophy, because she did not think philosophy was that at all.

Finally, one can also make a related mistake by thinking that in uncovering her "metaphysics" one has uncovered the ultimate grounds for everything else she has to say, that one has somehow gotten "behind" what she says to find something like a theory that explains her various positions, or that somehow causes them, or that somebody else could use to build an intellectual position. Such a theory, of course, would constitute the ultimate meaning of her philosophical work, and what she has to say as a whole would then stand or fall on that. But again this is not how she thought.

So, with these caveats, it will be helpful to turn to some of Weil's own striking comments to say what she does think philosophy *is*. Fortunately, we have not only suggestive isolated comments but also several essays and sets of notes from her most intellectually productive period that deal with the issue.

I

Initially, however, many of these comments, striking as they may be, do not appear very promising for development. For example, in a couple of places she posits that there are two traditions to which philosophers belong. One is the Platonic tradition, in which Weil also includes Descartes and Kant. The other, which she clearly disdains, includes Aristotle and Hegel. It is clear what in the latter tradition she wants to exclude from true philosophy. She says what it is. This is the tradition of system builders, the philosophers who "construct systems in order to eliminate contradiction."[2] These are those, who like Aristotle, seek for God by means of human reason but who ultimately fail at the wisdom of thinkers such as Plato.[3] The distinction she seems to be drawing is one between a sort of contemplative, even mystical version of philosophy and a sort of worldly rationalism. This is reinforced in her comments on method in philosophy at the opening of her London notebooks:

> The proper method of philosophy consists in clearly conceiving the insoluble problems in all their insolubility and then in simply contemplating them, fixedly and tirelessly, year after year, without any hope, patiently waiting.
> By this standard, there are few philosophers. And one can hardly even say a few.
> There is no entry into the transcendent until the human faculties — intelligence, will, human love — have come up against a limit, and the human being waits at this threshold, which he can make no move to cross, without turning away and without knowing what he wants, in fixed, unwavering attention.
> It is a state of extreme humiliation.
> Genius is the supernatural virtue of humility in the domain of thought. That is demonstrable.[4]

This is striking, but here it is much easier to say what Weil is *against* in philosophy than what she actually thinks true philosophy is. She thinks that any philosophy that is systematic to the degree that it thinks that it has an answer to everything or a universal method has missed the mark. Philosophy contemplates contradictions and the rough spots in human existence, it does not try to solve them and to smooth away difficulties. It looks, it asks, it does not prescribe. There is a general reason for this view. For, somewhat more positively, insofar as she has an eye on the transcendent, and on the search for God, it is clear that she thinks that doing philosophy like that is inadequate to its object. In part, this is because she does think the world as a whole gives evidence to a mystery that stands behind its existence and that penetrates it. This is everywhere evident in her later writings. Reason, which is a natural faculty, cannot penetrate and master this mystery, especially using language. Indeed, she is biting in pushing this point, as she does in the essay

"What Is Sacred in Every Human Being?" (chapter 6). There she argues that what any mind can conceive is limited by the number of relations it can hold, and there is a limit to that for even the most capacious of minds, a limit that falls far short of the relations that are in the world, and of any that are beyond language. She observes: "The difference between people more or less intelligent is like the difference between prisoners condemned to life in prison whose cells are more or less large. An intelligent man who is proud of his intelligence is like a prisoner who is proud of having a big cell."[5]

What the mind needs to do therefore is to contemplate the world, and to be revealed to; thinking that one has the world down as a system fails at understanding either the world or reason itself. Even theology, which begins in revelation, fails of its object when it tries to smooth out all the wrinkles. As she argues, often with great applause, "The gospel contains a conception of life, not a theology."[6]

That much is fairly clear and easily drawn out of her writings. But what is not so easy to say is what, therefore, philosophy *is*. She did think of philosophy very highly. But it is not at all clear yet what thinking is and it ought to be, even though it is evident that she believes that one ought to think, and to think hard and deeply. She hardly thinks of philosophy romantically, or as an exercise in irony, either.

A comparison may help in seeing what is at stake here and where she wants to go. In the *Philosophical Fragments*, Kierkegaard's pseudonymous author, Johannes Climacus, is trying to get at what Christianity is. His problem is like Weil's. Philosophy, at least of the sort that the Hegelians practice, fails of its object. Dialectic is not going to get at the concept of Christianity correctly. So the task for Climacus is twofold—to show where and how dialectic fails and to show what Christianity is in such a way that one does get the concept. With respect to the first, there are a number of issues. For example, at the outset he argues that whenever dialectic is practiced objectively, then *when* in one's life one acquired dialectical skill or *who* one's teacher was are irrelevant to the conclusion ultimately drawn from the dialectical exercise. But that is not the case with Christianity, where the teacher and the timing in one's life are crucial. There is something about the thinker herself, how she is situated, and the grace of the teacher that are at stake in getting the concept. Note carefully that the problem Climacus is outlining is not simply that there is an upper limit to dialectic or reason—it is not just that one is not smart enough, but if one were, then the answer would be forthcoming. With respect to the problem of what Christian faith is, the very essence of the concept has to do with the living natures of both the investigator and what she is thinking about. What is going on is a sort of understanding of the concept that requires putting it in proper context, and, in this case, this context also includes the spiritual and moral status of the inquirer. Climacus can see that much. What is beyond even him, though, is that when one has done a better job of grasping the concept of Christianity, as he has, even that falls short. Why? Because if understanding the concept fully involves the person intimately, Climacus, who is not a believer, still misses the idea by standing outside it. The full understanding of Christian faith may well be faith itself; if so, then simply seeing that it is so will only be half the game, at best—that advance may still be at the cost of what Weil called an "infinite error." But at least it is an important step to see that it does involve one subjectively, and to see the importance of such things as who one's teacher was and the proper time. To go further, though, and this is the point of the comparison, requires one to understand that something very different than dialectic is needed.

Weil does not always go down the same path with respect to that "something different." Kierkegaard, for example, tended to leave philosophy itself intact and use it as a sort of servant to religious understanding, pursuing religious understanding with an entirely different kind of authorship. Weil, on the other hand, tends to blend and order the two in such a way that she sees philosophy, rightly understood, as being central to that "something different." Part of that is in the distinctive way she sees philosophy. But at least where we have come to now is to have seen somewhat more of why she thinks that there is a difference between the sort of philosophy that produces views and arguments and the sort of philosophy where *how* one thinks is integrally involved with what one thinks, and conceptually so. That is a helpful advance. So, as far as Weil is concerned, the problem is not just one of the limits of the intellect and the largeness and the qualitative difference of transcendent subject matter. The practice and activity of philosophy is also of concern to her. The very concept of philosophy itself is at stake.

Fortunately, we do have something more than a collection of gnomic statements by Weil about philosophy, and more than just her early thesis on Descartes and the somewhat later notes taken by a student in her philosophy class in Roanne in 1933–1934, which have come down to us as *Lectures on Philosophy.*[7] After fleeing Paris on the last train out before the Germans marched in, Weil spent most of the next two years in Marseille (September 1940–May 1942). This was an extremely productive and active period for her. She participated in resistance activities, regularly visited the internment camps, worked for a period in the grape harvest in the Rhone valley, and began her intense discussions about Christianity with Father Joseph-Marie Perrin. Her writings were voluminous. They included the numerous essays she wrote for Father Perrin on the ancient Greeks, in good part to convince him that they did know something of Christian truth. She continued to write on social issues. But she also became involved with the Société d'études philosophiques de Marseille, organized by Gaston Berger, who was also the editor of the *Cahiers du Sud*. As a result of her involvement with this group, Weil was able to concentrate a number of writings on explicit philosophical issues, including essays that dealt directly with the nature of philosophy itself, and others that were closely related. Two of them, "Essay on the Concept of Reading" (chapter 1) and "Some Reflections on the Concept of Value" (chapter 2), are of particular importance, but they have only recently been widely available. A close examination of them will help give us what Weil thought philosophy is.

II

In the "Essay on the Concept of Reading," Weil seeks to define a concept that she calls "reading," which is concerned with how we inescapably read meaning in the world. The phenomenon of how and where we read has a great deal of subtlety to it. For example, she notes how the world grips us through sensation: we are punched, we are burned, we double over, we jerk our hand back. The world indeed grips us and we feel it, and whatever we feel is the direct result of the world. We have no doubt about it. What Weil finds interesting is how this same sense of being gripped by the world can come about, not by the world directly impressing itself on us, but through the meanings we see in the world, in how we read the world. She gives the example of two women reading a letter. One falls down in the course of reading it; her life will never be the same afterwards. The other does not change a bit. The letter informs each of them that her son has been killed. The difference in their reactions? One knows how to read and the other doesn't. In a similar way, Weil suggests, in our reading of the world we feel and believe that the world itself grabs us. If on a dark road, we see a man lurking behind a tree, we are afraid as soon as we see him. We have no choice in the matter. If suddenly we see that it is not a man at all, but just a branch, the fear dissolves immediately. The problem she then raises is how certain insignificant sensations, such as the black marks on a printed page that our eyes look at, can seize us as they do. In a stronger sense, the question is that we are constantly being gripped by an exterior world through the meanings that we read. Here is a "contradiction," she thinks. On the one hand, what we read seizes us as if it were utterly external; our mere musings and thought experiments do not provoke the same strong reaction in us. On the other hand, we also know that these meanings somehow come from us.

It is important to pay attention to Weil's distinction between what she is calling "reading" and what is simply thought. What she is not saying is that we first interpret something and then see it as that, as if there were a choice or act of will that plays a role, or as if there were some option in what we are seeing or as if we were consciously adopting a point of view. We don't imagine it. There are, of course, plenty of occasions in which that does happen. Deliberately adopting a point of view is a frequent classroom exercise and is at the heart of teaching; it is one that takes place in assessing what a work of art might mean. But in the sort of reading that Weil is highlighting, what happens is precisely what Wittgenstein in a similar discussion, one of how aspects of things are seen by us, notes, "we interpret it and *see* it as we *interpret* it."[8] Where this is philosophically interesting is that because there is such a sense of immediacy, and of the direct givenness of the world, we are tempted to give a realist's imprimatur on what we read. But that would be a mistake—despite the seeming guarantee that readings come with, they do depend on us. It would, however, be just as much a mistake, and perhaps even epistemologically incoherent, to suggest that these readings are just invented or unreal. To do so is to try to permeate what appears most real, what has the most prima facie evidence for being the world's touch, with a sense of unreality. Because what we read does

come with such a sense of reality itself, as Weil points out, this gives rise
to all sorts of philosophical disputes, because when we are reading we
are doing much more than just trying out a position to see if it fits or
not; when we read, nothing could seem clearer to us than what we are
reading is the case, pure and simple. Even more to the point, ethical
debates, because readings for Weil usually intimately involve one's sense
of the good, become intractable — and particularly fierce. It is also where
academic debate, unsurprisingly to those who understand the nature of
reading, can be largely irrelevant to ethical decision making. She points
out: "A man who is tempted to keep a deposit for himself, will not keep
it simply because he has read *The Critique of Practical Reason*; he will
refrain from it, because it will seem to him, despite himself, that something in the deposit itself cries out to be given back."[9]

Weil is not particularly concerned to chase down where exactly our
readings come from. She is more interested in how they are changed, but
the answer to that question also says where, in general, they come from.
Perception and our attendant thought is not, as she first suggested in her
1930 dissertation "Science et perception dans Descartes," constructed
out of an undifferentiated mass of sensations. Instead, she recognizes
now that our readings are a part of what might be called our natural
history, including our bodily reactions and cultural and individual historical factors, for it is by similar factors that they can be changed. For
example, there is something about human beings where we simply read
a certain kind of respect due to them whenever we see them. We do not
deduce this respect from principles or from appearances of one kind or
another, or from the suggestion that there is a something in a human
being that by its presence demands we should not kill another or harm
her. We do not argue ourselves into not harming her. Yet, Weil also
notes, that in, say, a civil war, suddenly the very idea of *sparing* a human
being from death is weak and has to come from inside us. Force has
caused us to see the universe very differently than we did the day before.
The art of war is the art of changing people's readings.

Yet, she argues, we are not simply passive with respect to our readings. We do have a certain power over the way the universe grips us. If
we are wired for fear when a snake or a lion appears, we can also, as
the ancient Stoics and early Desert Fathers knew very well, do something about how we see things. If reading has a forceful emotional

component, our emotions themselves can be altered so that they read the world differently. We can learn not to be afraid. However, we cannot do this simply by thinking or wishing to see things differently. We cannot talk ourselves into it. Really to change requires an apprenticeship, she says, and this includes a bodily component. It also requires a regime of attention. It is because an apprenticeship can change our readings, including our relationship with the universe as a whole, that Weil is particularly concerned in her last writings with labor and social structure, things that do apprentice the souls subjected to them, for better or for worse. We learn to read in a certain way because of the way that we live. We also make use of what the world has to use for spiritual and moral transformation.

This brings us much closer to the question of what exactly philosophy is for Simone Weil. We can change our readings of the world, and throughout her later writings, whenever Weil talks about changing readings, and about apprenticeship, she is particularly concerned with our readings as moral readings and how we are related to the world as a whole. She generally divides the way that we read the universe into three sorts of readings. At the first level, we simply read the world from an utterly egocentric position. What is good is what pleases us and what gives us pleasure; what is evil is what hurts us and frustrates us. Things are read utterly egocentrically here. At the second level, we see things from a perspective where all things happen with equal importance; we see that they happen according to a rigorous order, and that the order's goodness does not depend upon us. We see ourselves as part of this larger order. So, what pleases us is not better than what pleases others and frustrates us. This is a sort of Stoic acceptance of the world; it is not one of resignation, but of positive acceptance. It is something that science should foster, even though scientists individually may talk and calculate one way professionally and then be utterly petty and self-centered in every other aspect of what they do. If so, they are theorizing one way, but actually reading another. Finally, at the highest level, what goes on in the world, as far as we read it, goes on as if we ourselves had positively willed it the way that we will a pencil to move along a sheet of paper; we don't first think about it and will all the intermediate steps, we just see and feel the paper. The ascending hierarchy of readings that Weil proposes is then like this: "to read necessity behind sensations, to read order behind necessity, to read God behind order."[10] We never escape reading, since as finite beings we always have a perspective (God alone does not read because God does not have a perspective), but it is possible to read God's goodness in all phenomena, and to take joy in them, and we can even assent to the things that may cause us sorrow as part of a good creation. Thus, she describes faith itself "as a gift of reading."[11]

III

What ought, however, to philosophically concern us most here is the question of the possibility of establishing anything like this kind of order to reading. This question, as Weil makes clear at the outset of the essay "Some Reflections on the Concept of Value," is the heart of what philosophy is, for philosophy, she claims, is the reflection on value that establishes an order among our values. More exactly, she argues, "all reflection bearing on the notion of value and on the hierarchy of values is philosophical; all efforts of thought bearing on anything other than value are, if one examines them closely, foreign to philosophy."[12] This is more than the sort of paradox and hyperbole Weil indulges in from time to time. It goes to the heart of the nature of philosophical thinking. For philosophy does not just think *about* the concept of value, in the way one might analyze any other subject; in this regard it does not produce results with respect to this as subject matter. Philosophy's thinking, which is purely reflective, is the thinking and reflecting on value. For, as she observes, value is not empirical; it is strictly a matter of reflection. In this regard, philosophy's own value is itself "beyond discussion" in much the same way, one might suggest, as the standard meter in Paris is beyond measurement. That is to say, it assesses value and is the principle of assessment, and that distinguishes it from what is assessed; there is no way of thinking in order to assess *its* value. The question simply disappears.

It is not hard to say why this is so, for Weil locates the reason within human life itself. Whatever we do implies a choice of values, and we are never without values. How this is so also means that our thinking about values, and hence philosophy itself, is conducted in a way that is quite unlike any search for knowledge. Whereas the search for knowledge of some thing depends upon the use of other knowledge that we have, and the result of our search is then as probable as our current knowledge is—and we know that it changes, which is the adventure of thinking—that simply is not the case with values. Because we are committed to certain values, and this commitment directs our reflections, we cannot and do not look at and treat those values as merely probable. We regard them as certain. As she points out, whatever values we have are not accepted conditionally or provisionally, to be adopted if reason makes them likely; no, they are purely and simply accepted, and are unconditional. In this sense, she says, values are unknowable, a proposition deliberately paradoxical but quite capable of explication. To say that values are unknowable is to say something relative to how knowledge of other things is arrived at, and that sort of knowledge is not how it works with values. The claim really is something more like a grammatical statement about the concept of value in our thinking. The concept of value works differently and plays a different role in our thinking than concepts respecting the gaining of knowledge play.

Weil, however, in her essay does seem to want to continue to play things out under the guise of the paradox in order to give some further sense of what values are, and how our thinking is inescapably directed by them, and not understandable without them. So, she asks, if values are unknowable, then why not give up on them? Well, we simply don't. We always live life in a directed way, which is the playing out of value. (If anyone does not live in such a way, say, in the case of affliction, or severe mental disease, the fact is therefore diagnostic of a pathology, not a disqualifying exception.) Thus she says, "at the center of human life is a contradiction."[13] This is again deliberately paradoxical, but in a very Weilian way. When Weil uses the term "contradiction" she is usually broadly pointing at what might be better specified as a tension, or, even more accurately, as conceptual incommensuration. This is the case here, as she argues that the concept of knowledge, which we would like to employ with respect to values in order to know how to judge between them, simply is not going to fly. Assuming mistakenly that it is the way to go, though, we think that we are stymied. And it appears that we would have to go this way, because we need to know how values are related. So there is at least a tension, or, rhetorically, a contradiction, or, best of all, two different grammars facing us. But, despite this, as Weil then goes on, values still operate in our thinking; however, not as easily and clearly articulated concepts, but, again, more like the way that a standard for measuring that cannot itself be measured might operate.

In a helpful analogy, she suggests that the situation is like that of an aesthetic standard for an artist. It is not just that she knows what she likes, even if she can't exactly say why. It is that she judges her own works as better or worse, and does so unavoidably. We have a standard, we apply it rigorously, but we also know that somehow *in concreto* it has been realized only in a very imperfect way. (Weil seems to have had a similar idea in mind in the essay "At the Price of an Infinite Error: The Scientific Image, Ancient and Modern" [chapter 10] when she talks about how we reason using perfect geometrical relations, even though we apply them to, and have them suggested to us by, very imperfect straight lines that are drawn on blackboards or on paper.)

Weil wants to keep our minds focused on this problem, and she quickly rejects the suggestion that we maybe should stand back and ask whether we even ought to think about values: perhaps, since thinking about them is so messy, they are just fictions. That tack, she thinks, is nonsensical, an example of what Wittgenstein called "language going on holiday." Of course, we can ask the question insofar as we can put the words together, and in other contexts, putting this kind of question together is the right thing to do. But in this case, we cannot stand outside ourselves that way; we always strive towards value, and we would have to undercut our very selves actually to doubt that concept of value.

So, what does this mean for knowing the relative order of values? In one sense, she says very surprisingly, it means that "the rigor and certitude of philosophical investigation are as great as they can be; the sciences don't come close."[14] Philosophical reflection is infallible. What Weil seems to have in mind here is that when we do reflect on values, we simply deduce the relative order in relation to the chief values we hold, and we are in no position to doubt it, since that would mean not holding certain values at the same time that we do hold them. But, Weil continues, we do so in a way that now moves to take seriously the problem posed by the other side of the equation, namely, the problem that ranking values this way poses, the question we have to ask when we are told that ranking values is, purely and simply, nothing more than tracing the chain of one's own thoughts. In that case, to recommend them universally, and values are held as being universally true, is then just advocacy. So, why are they not just us, the expression of our readings, and why not count our readings as purely subjective? What has been missing here is not, however, the concept of knowledge, which we would like to clear things up but which is actually causing all the problems. What has been missing, or, rather, the concept that has lain hidden in the background, she thinks, is the concept of detachment. The problem, she argues, is not that we are certain about values—that is part of the grammar of values; the problem is that we need somehow to detach our very personal and private interests from our thinking about value if we are going to do philosophy, if we are actually going to reflect. Detachment is the crucial moral value that gives value to reflection, for it puts narrow self-interest aside. That, of course, would seem to make philosophical reflection impossible, because it would mean that whenever we are trying to be detached, we are at the same time trying to run out a chain of reasoning based on our striving for some other value. The striving for detachment might win, of course, but only if we see it as the superior value; but to do that, we would have to quit striving in life in the way we have been.

Weil suggests that this makes genuine philosophical reflection pretty much a miracle, and even more so given that we suffer under the illusion that our reflections are detached from our personal interests and goals much more than they really are. But, putting aside for a moment how it comes about, we are now actually in a position to say what philosophy is. Philosophy seeks a ranking to value. But in trying to find the truth of this ranking, since value is not an abstract consideration external to our living, one, in order to do philosophy, has to be willing to renounce the idea of one's own projects as all-important. One has to detach self, at least a certain sense of self, from the thought. That is what in concrete terms detachment means, and "this is why in the ancient mysteries, in Platonism, [etc.], detachment has always been compared to death, and the initiation into wisdom has been regarded as a sort of passage towards death."[15] But that also means, therefore, that philosophical reflection has as its goal not knowledge, but transformation. Philosophical reflection is the giving over of oneself to reality. It begins and has its being in that willingness to begin anew, and to take otherness into itself and give itself to a world not of its own making.

What she says in a letter to Father Perrin about herself when she talks about her intellectual vocation follows quite naturally from this, namely, that she believes her thought should "be indifferent to all ideas without exception" and that her mind with respect to ideas ought to be like water, which is indifferent to the objects that fall into it: "It does not weigh them; they weigh themselves after a certain time of oscillation."[16]

It is here a number of Weil's claims about philosophy have a sense that they may not have had at first glance, such as that philosophy is not a matter of accumulating knowledge and that it does not concern itself with contradictions. There also may be some additional sense to the ancient tradition of philosophy that she cites so approvingly and that includes such disparate figures as Plato, Descartes, Kant, Lagneau, Alain, and Husserl. At first blush, Descartes and Kant, to name just the two most obvious ones on the list, could not seem further from such a conception of philosophy. But what Weil seems to have in mind as being genuinely philosophical in them is not what they are best known for: the quest for certainty of the "I think therefore I am," or the quest for an infallible method, or the architectonic of the *Critique of Pure Reason*. Rather, if we consider what she says in her brief review "Philosophy" (written at the same time; chapter 3 herein), where she again cites Descartes and Kant as examples of genuine philosophy, we discover that genuine philosophy consists in asking what an idea means, not whether it is true or false. Philosophers who think this way are oriented towards salvation, she adds.[17]

The historical insight is, I suppose, arguable, but it is not really what is at stake for her or for her reader in the claim. The simple connection of philosophy as asking what things mean with salvation, with saving one's life, and then opposing it to building a beautiful system with everything in its place, is an astounding insight. It could even be life-changing if it were taken seriously and at its greatest depth; it at least ought to make us read philosophers in a different way. But, in any case, what we can now see is that what is above all crucial to philosophy for Weil is that it is a practice, a transformation of the self, of the thinker, an inquiry about value while holding a certain value. Weil clearly held this view to the end. In what is nearly her last notebook entry before her death, Weil returns to the subject of philosophy:

Philosophy (including problems of cognition, etc.) is *exclusively* an affair of action and practice. That is why it is so difficult to write about it. Difficult in the same way as a treatise on tennis or running, but much more so.

Subjectivist theories of cognition are a perfectly correct description of the condition of those who lack the faculty, which is extremely rare, of coming out of themselves.

A supernatural faculty.

Charity.[18]

In suggesting that philosophy is an affair of action and practice, and comparing writing on it to writing a treatise on tennis or running, Weil means that to do philosophy is a matter of one's own action and practice. The sort of detachment she insists is crucial to it is a matter of how one lives life. It is not simply a method to produce philosophical treatises.

IV

At this point many of the far more familiar outlines of Weil's other writings come into view once again. Tracing them and pondering them is best left here as an exercise for her reader, who will benefit far more from thinking them out than from having them presented as if they were philosophical products. However, I would like to mention one place where Weil's understanding, and self-understanding, of what it means to be a philosopher opens out. To bring this to mind is one final effort to deepen what is at stake. That is the connection of Weil's reflections on value and philosophy and her concept of attention.

Weil's concept of attention is famously laid out in her essay, also from the Marseille period, "Reflections on the Right Use of School Studies with a View to the Love of God." There, in a marvelously succinct essay written for school girls, she notes that the value of intellectual work is the development of attention. She defines attention as consisting in "suspending our thought, leaving it available (*disponible*), empty, and penetrable by the object."[19] This concept and its analogues in other writings in such concepts as the divine emptying (*kenosis*), patience, waiting, contemplation, and detachment are key to Weil's overall thought in a way that perhaps no other set of concepts is. That set of related concepts is crucial for letting Weil move around in moral, spiritual, and intellectual problems in the way that she does, and it is what gives them the sort of character that she thinks they have. In this respect, it may not be too much to say that for her the relation of various subject matters, say, such as philosophy and religious faith, is the relation of the various grammars of this set of concepts in the world. For example, as she makes clear in the "School Studies" essay, intellectual attention used in such minor things as paying attention to a difficult geometrical problem may bloom ultimately into prayer. Prayer may turn ultimately into waiting. The ability to look at one's neighbor and to see a human being in one who is afflicted is also a matter of moral attention, as is the ability to perceive the beauty of the universe as a whole.

But a warning is in order. It is important to see how Weil can move so consistently and insightfully among these fields of activity and inquiry, and this set of related concepts allows that. It is equally important to keep two things in mind while she does move around them. The first is that these are related concepts, but they are not necessarily the same concept; at the very least, how they operate is dependent on context. Frequently that is because there are different levels to life and thought; at least Weil thought so, a point that is crucial to understanding Weil's writing. Intellectual work, for example, which demands detachment, is not the same thing as religious faith, which demands a far deeper availability to God, and an even more radical detachment to the things of this world; even faith comes at different levels. So, although both philosophy and faith require a certain distance from the self, at certain points, however, they may also conflict. The example of her own life is clear enough on how this can happen. In her debates with priests about baptism and joining the community of faith, Weil is quite clear that the sense of detachment that she is adamant about with respect to intellectual work does keep her out of the Church. Why? In part, because the Church has a much different sense of philosophy, that is, as something that produces certain metaphysical results that, it thinks, should undergird the claims of faith. Since she is willing to entertain contrary propositions, she feels she would be compromising her intellectual vocation to join the Church. Yet, at the same time, she says, and clearly understands, that the demands of faith do not necessarily defeat intellectual work. Faith is an object of love, not intellect. The Church, she thinks, needs therefore to propose doctrine to love and attention, and it should not confuse things by making love and attention an issue of the intellect that operates at a lower level. There is much more that can be said about this issue, and has been said, but the point is clear enough. These matters are on different levels. Ultimately, she herself did not think they conflicted, but she also did not easily see a way to where they did not finally conflict for her as she stood at that point. Thus, it is quite right to say that, ultimately, the lower sort of attention paid to school problems might apprentice one to prayer, and in the end, one might pray and live *en hupomene*, "in patient waiting and endurance." But to someone who lives at one level, and not another, even if she can suspect some kind of reconciliation intellectually, the problem remains, and it is a real one. I suggest that is what Weil came to think is the very form of a real philosophical problem. But in this case, philosophy may also be a help. For if it contemplates this sort of problem, with a willingness and desire for transformation, it may well be an important part of the transformation of the thinker.

The second thing to keep in mind follows from this. Where any of these concepts conflict, or move towards each other, cannot, for Weil, be put outside of how they conflict or are resolved in life.[20] One can put words together to question whether there is value or not, but doing so is senseless, because we as thinkers seek purpose; the conflicts and resolutions to problems of value, and other problems, also, need to be thought in relation to what Wittgenstein called "the rough ground." These are the problems of active thinkers, who themselves live life at some very different levels and in some very different ways. That does not let the thinker off the hook. It does require that where the contradiction needs to be understood and where resolution needs to take place is in the lived context, where the contradictions are not smoothed over, and where the peace gained thereby is the peace of the thinker, not the consistency of the written thought.

The Center of Theological Inquiry
Princeton, New Jersey

NOTES

1. Miklos Vetö, *The Religious Metaphysics of Simone Weil*, trans. Joan Dargan (Albany: State University Press of New York, 1994) (French original, 1971).

2. "Some Reflections on the Concept of Value," in this volume.

3. See "God in Plato," in this volume.

4. Simone Weil, *First and Last Notebooks* (Oxford: Oxford University Press, 1970), 335.

5. "What Is Sacred in Every Human Being?," in this volume.

6. Weil, *First and Last Notebooks*, 147.

7. Simone Weil, *Lectures on Philosophy*, trans. Hugh Price (Cambridge: Cambridge University Press, 1978) (French original, 1959).

8. Ludwig Wittgenstein, *Philosophical Investigations*, rev. 4th ed., trans. G. E. M. Anscombe, P. M. S. Hacker, and Joachim Schulte (Chichester: Wiley-Blackwell, 2009), xi.116.

9. "Essay on the Concept of Reading," in this volume.

10. Simone Weil, *The Notebooks of Simone Weil*, trans. A. Wills (London: Routledge & Kegan Paul, 1956), 266–67.

11. Ibid., 220.

12. "Some Reflections on the Concept of Value," in this volume.

13. Ibid.

14. Ibid.

15. Ibid.

16. Simone Weil, *Waiting for God*, trans. Emma Craufurd (New York: Harper and Row, 1973), 85.

17. "Philosophy," in this volume.

18. Weil, *First and Last Notebooks*, 362.

19. My translation. See Weil, *Waiting for God*, 111.

20. I think this is why in her own teaching of philosophy, Weil began to use literature extensively. This was not a matter of illustrating philosophical problems for young, unsophisticated minds who could not grasp difficult abstractions. Rather, the problem is always in the specific concrete relations.

CHAPTER ONE

Essay on the Concept of Reading

(Essai sur la notion de lecture)

This essay was written in the spring of 1941. While it appears that Weil had plans to expand it at some future date, the present form of the essay is already the result of much previous thinking, as her notebooks show many forays into the concept. The concept of reading also appears in other essays of this period and later. As it is, the essay is in a largely finished state, Weil's mother having typed it, and her typescript has Weil's comments on it. The essay appeared in *Les Études philosophiques*, a journal founded by Gaston Berger, in 1946. The notion of reading that Weil develops here does not seem to be in response to any other thinker; it is original to her.

We shall attempt to define a concept that has not yet found a suitable name, but for which the name "reading" may be the best one. For there is a mystery in reading, a mystery that, if we contemplate it, may well help us, not to explain, but to grab hold of other mysteries in human life.

All of us know that sensation is immediate, a brute fact, and that it seizes us by surprise. Without warning a man is punched in the stomach; everything changes for him before he even knows what happened. I touch something hot and I jerk my hand back before I even know that I burned myself. Something seizes me here—it is the universe, and I recognize it by the way it treats me. No one is surprised by the power that punches, burns, or sudden noises have to grab hold of us, for we know, or at least believe, that they come from outside us, from matter, and that the mind does not play any part in the sensation, except to submit to it. The thoughts that we ourselves form may bring on certain emotions, but we are not seized by them in the same way.

The mystery is that there are sensations that are pretty much insignificant in themselves, yet, by what they signify, what they mean, they seize us in the same way as the stronger sensations. There are some black marks on a sheet of white paper; they couldn't differ more from a punch in the stomach. Yet, they can have the same effect. We have all experienced, to a greater or lesser degree, the effect of bad news that we have read in a letter or newspaper. Before we have fully taken account of what is going on, we feel ourselves seized and thrown down just as if we had been hit; even much later the sight of the letter remains painful. Sometimes, when time has lessened the pain a bit, one is shuffling through papers and suddenly the letter jumps out, an even more stabbing pain surfaces, just as piercing as any physical pain, seizing us as if it came from outside ourselves and as if the letter itself were on fire. Two women each receive a letter saying that her son is dead. The first one glances at it, faints, and until the day she dies her eyes, her mouth, and her movements will never again be the same. The second one remains unmoved; her face, her posture do not change at all: she doesn't know how to read. It isn't the sensation, it is the meaning that has seized the first woman by striking her mind, immediately, as a brute fact, without her participation in the matter, just the way that sensations strike us. Everything happens as if the pain were in the letter itself, and jumped out from the letter to land on the face reading it. With respect to the actual sensations themselves—the color of the paper or the ink—they do not even come to mind. It is the pain that is given to one's sight.

Thus at each instant of our life we are gripped from the outside, as it were, by meanings that we ourselves read in appearances. That is why we can argue endlessly about the reality of the external world, since what we call the world are the meanings that we read; they are not real. But they seize us as if they were external; that is real. Why should we try to resolve this contradiction when the more important task of thought in this world is to define and contemplate insoluble contradictions, which, as Plato said, draw us upwards?

What is peculiar here is that what we are given is not sensations *and* meanings; what we read is alone what is given. Studies of eyewitness accounts have notably shown this. Proofreading is difficult because while reading we often see letters that the typesetters have actually forgotten to put in; one has to force oneself to read a different kind of meaning here, not that of words or phrases, but of mere letters, while still not forgetting that the first kind of meaning exists. It is impossible not to read; we cannot look at a printed text in a language we understand that is placed in front of us and not read it. At best, one could do this only after a lot of practice.

The "blind man's stick," a favorite example of Descartes, furnishes an image analogous to reading. Everybody can convince himself that when handling a pen his touch goes right through the pen to the nib. If the pen skips because of some problem with the paper, the *pen's* skipping is what is immediately felt; we don't even think about the sensations in our fingers or hand through which we read. However, the pen's skipping is really only something we read. The sky, the sea, the sun, the stars, human beings, everything that surrounds us is in the same way something that we read. What we call a correction of a sensory illusion is actually a modified reading. If at night, on a lonely road, I think I see a man waiting in ambush instead of what is actually a tree, it is a human and menacing presence that forces itself on me, and, as in the case of the letter, it makes me quiver even before I know what it is. I get closer and suddenly everything changes, and as I read a tree, and not a man, I no longer quiver. There is not an appearance *and* then an interpretation; a human presence has penetrated to my soul through my eyes, and now, just as suddenly, the presence of a tree. If I hate someone, he is not on one side and my hatred on the other; when he comes near me it is odiousness itself that approaches; the perversity of his soul is more evident to me than the color of his hair. Moreover, if he is blond, he is a hateful blond, if he is a brunette, he is a hateful brown. Esther in drawing near to Ahasuerus did not draw near to a man who she knew could put her to death; she drew near to majesty itself, to terror itself that reaches her soul through her eyes; that is why the very effort of walking towards him makes her stumble. She herself says so; what she looks at with fear is not the face of Ahasuerus, it is the majesty that is etched there, and she reads that. We speak generally in such cases of the effects of the imagination, but it may well be better to use the word "reading." This word implies that it is a question of effects produced by appearances. However, they are appearances that do not actually appear, or hardly ever; what does appear is something else that is related to appearances as a phrase is related to letters. We see it as an appearance, suddenly, as a brute fact, from outside, and, according to the evidence, pretty much irrefutably.

If I see a book bound in black, except to philosophize, I do not doubt that black is there. If I look at the top of a newspaper and see "June 14," I do not doubt that it was printed on June 14. If a being that I hate, or that I fear, or that I despise, or that I love approaches, I above all do not doubt that I have in front of me the odious, the dangerous, the despicable, the lovable. If someone, reading the same newspaper and looking at the same place in it, seriously told me, after several tries, that he did not read "June 14" but "June 15," that would bother me. I wouldn't know what to say. If someone does not hate, fear, despise, or love the way I do, that also bothers me. How? He sees these beings — or, if they are distant, he sees the indirect manifestations of their existence — and he does not read the odious, the dangerous, the despicable, the lovable? That is not possible. This is a case of bad faith; he's lying; he's crazy. It is not quite right to say that we believe ourselves in danger because we are afraid; on the contrary, we are afraid because of the presence of danger since it is danger that gives rise to fear. However, danger *is* something that I read. Sounds and sights are by themselves devoid of danger, they are no more dangerous than the paper and the ink in a threatening letter. But in the case of a threatening letter the danger that I read takes me beyond those things, and makes fear come to me. If I hear an explosion, fear lives in the noise and comes to take my soul by hearing; I no more can refuse to fear than I can refuse to hear. If I know what the sound is, the same thing happens when I hear the "ack-ack" of a machine gun; it doesn't if I don't know. It is not, however, a question of something that is analogous to a conditioned reflex; it is a question of something analogous to *reading*, where sometimes a combination of novel signs that I have never seen seizes my soul right where the wounding meaning penetrates, along with the black and the white, and just as irresistibly.

Thus meanings, which if looked at abstractly would seem to be mere thoughts, arise from every corner around me, taking possession of my soul and shaping it from one moment to the next in such a way that, to borrow a familiar English phrase, "my soul is no longer my own." I believe what I read, my judgments are what I read, I act according to what I read; how could I act any other way? If I read in a noise honor to be won, I run towards the noise; if I read danger and nothing else, I run far from the noise. In both cases, the necessity of acting the way I do, even if I regret it, is imposed on me in a clear and immediate way, as the noise, with the noise. I read in the noise. In the same way, if during civil unrest or war unarmed men are sometimes killed, it is because there is something vile about these beings that penetrates through the eyes to the soul of armed men along with the sight of their clothes, hair, faces, something that asks to be annihilated. In a glance, these armed men read along with their hair color and flesh the evidence that says it is necessary to kill them. If in the normal course of life there are actually few crimes, it is because we read in the colors that penetrate our eyes that when a human being is standing in front of us that there is something to which we owe a certain measure of respect. It is the same thing as with the case of the man who, on a lonely road, first sees a man looking out for passersby, and then a tree. It is in the first case above all an unreserved response to a human presence, and the idea that there could be a *question* of a man is an abstract one that is weak and that comes from within him, not from the outside, and that has no bite. Then suddenly is triggered within him, without transition, the fact that he is alone, surrounded only by plants and things. The idea that a man could have been there where he now sees a tree has become in its turn a weak idea. In the same way, during peacetime, the idea of causing the death of a human being comes from the inside, it isn't read in the appearances—one reads, on the contrary, in the appearances the prohibition of killing. But in a civil war, put somebody in contact with a certain category of human beings and the idea of *sparing* a life is weak, coming from the inside. There is no transition possible in going from one state to the other; the passage happens as by the pulling of a trigger. Each reading, when it is current, appears as the only real, only possible way to look at things; the other one seems purely imaginary. These are, of course, extreme examples, but all of our life is made from the same cloth; meanings impose themselves on us successively, and each of them, when it appears and enters into us through the senses, reduces all opposing ideas to the status of phantoms.

I possess a certain power over the universe that allows me to change appearances, but it is an indirect one that requires work; it isn't there by simply wishing. I put a sheet of white paper over a black book and I no longer see black. This power is limited by the limits of my physical strength. I also possibly possess a certain power to change the meanings that I read in appearances and that are imposed on me. However, this power is also limited, indirect, and it, too, requires work. Labor in the normal sense of the word is an example of this work because every tool is a blind man's stick, an instrument for reading, and every apprenticeship is an apprenticeship in reading. When the apprenticeship ends, meanings come to me from the nib of my pen or from a phrase embedded in printed characters. For the sailor, for the experienced captain, his boat has become in a sense an extension of his own body; it is an instrument by which to read the tempest, and he reads it very differently than a passenger does. Where the passenger reads chaos and unlimited danger, the captain reads necessities, limited dangers, resources for escaping, and an obligation to be courageous and honorable.

Action on oneself and action on others consist in transforming meanings. A man, a head of state, declares war, and new meanings rise up all round forty million people. The general's art is to lead enemy soldiers into reading flight in appearances and in such a way that the idea of holding fast loses all substance, all effectiveness. He can do it, for example, by stratagems, by surprises, by using new weapons. War, politics, eloquence, art, teaching, all action on others essentially consists in changing what they read.

Whether it is a question of action on oneself or another, there are two issues to deal with, that of technique and that of value. Texts, whose appearances are characters, take hold of my soul, then abandon it and are replaced by others. Is one worth more than the other? Is one truer than the other? Where does one find a norm? Thinking a text to be true even though I am not reading it, that I have never read it, assumes that there is a reader of this truthful text, which is to say, it assumes God. But as soon as we do that, there is a contradiction, for the concept of reading does not fit our concept of God. Even if it did, it still would not let us order our readings of texts according to a scale of values.

Still, posed this way, the problem would perhaps be worth meditating on. For posed in this way it presents in one package all the possible problems of value, to the degree that they are concrete. A man who is tempted to keep a deposit for himself will not keep from doing it simply because he has read *The Critique of Practical Reason*; he will refrain from it, because it will seem to him, despite himself, that something in the deposit itself cries out to be given back. Everybody has experienced something like this where it seems that one would actually like to act badly, but cannot do it. At other times, one would like to act well, but one cannot do it. Figuring out whether one who reads returning a deposit this way reads better than someone who reads in the appearances all the desires that he might be able to satisfy if he kept the money is to seek for a criterion that would allow one to decide the matter, to seek out a technique that would permit one to pass from one reading to another. That is a problem that is more concrete than trying to decide whether it is better to keep it or give it back. Furthermore, by posing the problem of value this way around the concept of reading puts it in relation to truth and beauty as well as to the good, and it is not possible to separate them. Perhaps doing this, the connection of these three things, which is a mystery, would be made a bit clearer. We do not know how to think these things as one, and yet they cannot be thought separately.

CHAPTER TWO

Some Reflections on the Concept of Value

On Valéry's Claim That Philosophy Is Poetry

(*Quelques réflexions autour de la notion de valeur*)

This unfinished essay was written in the early months of 1941. The context of the essay is a series of lectures that the poet Paul Valéry gave in the Collège de France between 1937 and 1945. Notes taken by a listener from the opening lecture were published in the journal *Yggdrasil* in December 1937. Weil had read these notes. Her reading prompted a letter to Valéry, some entries in her notebooks, and finally this essay. Weil responds particularly to Valéry's claim that "philosophy is poetry," which she quotes at the end of the essay. Valéry had suggested in his first lecture that with respect to a value of a work of art there is an economic analogy in the relations of the author, the text, and the reader and those of the producer, product, and consumer. Weil saw this as "instructive" insofar as he was able to give voice to the subtle character of spiritual value without ultimately reducing it to economic value, but ultimately she saw the analogy as insufficient. In later lectures, Valéry goes on to ridicule the grand philosophical systems, while continuing to make use of the economic analogy. Weil comments on this at the end of this essay, very significantly stressing that given the nature of value in the philosophical quest, producing a system is actually foreign to the heart of philosophy.

The concept of value is at the center of philosophy. All reflection bearing on the notion of value and on the hierarchy of values is philosophical; all efforts of thought bearing on anything other than value are, if one examines them closely, foreign to philosophy. For that reason the value of philosophy itself is beyond discussion. For, as a matter of fact, the notion of value is always present to everybody's mind. Everybody orients his thoughts about action towards some good, and no one can do otherwise. Moreover, value is exclusively an object of reflection. It cannot be an object of experience. In a sense, the law of human life is: since the choice of life is one between life and death, then first, reflecting about and then living in any specific situation itself implies a choice of values. It is true, of course, that people almost never direct their thought to the values that they live by. But that is because they believe that they have reason enough for holding the ones they do.

Knowing how to judge between values is for everybody the supreme necessity. But it is also something that no one will ever find out. That is because all human knowledge is hypothetical; that is, the certainty of demonstrations rests on previous demonstrations or axioms, and the facts that one affirms, thanks to physical sense, are only admitted insofar as they are linked to other facts. But value cannot be a matter for hypothesis. A value is something that one admits unconditionally. At each instant our life is oriented according to some system of values. At the moment when it directs our actions, our system of values is not accepted with conditions or provisionally or reflectively; it is purely and simply accepted. Knowledge is conditional, values are unconditional; therefore values are unknowable.

But one cannot give up on knowing them, for giving up would mean giving up on believing in them, which is impossible, because human life always has a direction. Thus at the center of human life is a contradiction.

These considerations seem abstract because of the difficulty of expressing them in words. Nevertheless, this contradiction continually constitutes under diverse forms the essential drama of every human being, and it is easy to give as many concrete examples of it as one wants. For example, every artist knows that he cannot have an explicit criterion that lets him affirm with certitude whether one work of art is more beautiful than another. However, every artist also knows that there is a hierarchy of aesthetic values, that there are some things more beautiful than others, and that there are some things that are beautiful and others that are not. If he didn't know that, he wouldn't make the effort to do artistic work, to correct a work, or to continue working. The condition of the artist striving always towards a beauty he cannot know mixes anguish into every effort of artistic creation. But this condition is not just true of artists — it holds for everyone analogously.[1]

Everything that can be taken as an end cannot be defined. Means, such as power or money, are easily defined, and that is why people orient themselves exclusively towards the acquisition of means. But they then fall into another contradiction, for there is a contradiction of taking means for ends.

By transposition, one finds an analogous contradiction in every human situation. Hence, it is inevitable that all philosophic thought equally has a contradiction at its center. The logical rule of non-contradiction is not applicable in philosophy.

What else can a mind that would establish an order among values ask? Ought it to respond to the question: "Can we be sure that things have a value?" [or, similarly,] "Is everything equally without value?" Such questions are devoid of sense, not only because there is no method by which to search for an answer, but for a more profound reason. The ability to pose such a question rests entirely on the ability to put together words. But the mind cannot really pose this question to itself, it cannot truly be uncertain about whether the notion of value is or is not something fictional. For the mind essentially and always, in whatever manner it is disposed, strives towards value. It cannot regard the notion of value itself as uncertain, without regarding its own existence as uncertain, and that is impossible.

With respect to the order of values, established by reflection, what uncertainty can one raise on this subject? The primary value of the order by itself keeps one from raising any doubts. For as soon as I recognize an order to my thoughts, such that the value of a certain judgment is the condition for the value of all the others, excepting those that came before it and that I knew, what more can I ask? Can I suppose some other idea, which I don't recognize, is truer than those that I have just classified, and which might contradict them? No, for a comparison of value between two ideas implies one and the same mind that thinks both. The assumed idea ought therefore to be conceived as capable of being thought by me. But then I would conceive it as being classified in the hierarchy of ideas, after the first ones, and it would not have any more value than they do. Since value is a character of my thought, the hierarchy that I see between values is certain; nothing exterior to my thought can intervene in the notion of value. And to see why that matters, it is necessary to remember that truth is a value of thought. The word "truth" cannot have any other meaning.

Thus the rigor and the certitude of philosophical investigation are as great as they can be: the sciences don't come close. Do we then have to conclude that philosophical reflection is infallible? Yes, if we actually engaged in it. But human nature renders philosophical reflection pretty much impossible. For since the mind is always straining towards some value, how can it stand back, detaching itself from the value towards which it is moving in order to consider and judge it, and to rank it in relation to other values? This detachment demands an effort, and every effort of the mind strives towards a value. Thus in order to make this effort of detachment, the mind has to regard this detachment as the supreme value. But in order to see detachment as the superior value, it is already necessary to be detached from all the other values. So there is a vicious circle here that makes the exercise of reflection look like a miracle. The word "grace" expresses this miraculous character. The *illusion* of detachment, however, is frequent, since one often mistakes a simple change of values for detachment.

An athlete in the heat of the contest, breathless and agonized, doesn't ask himself why he wants to win, or to what degree he is right in wanting to win. He can't ask that of himself. After some hours of the agony of the contest, this question will then dawn on him: but this isn't detachment, it is simply that because of his exhaustion, rest and not gain has become valuable to him. The detachment needed for philosophical reflection consists in being detached, not only towards the values one has adopted beforehand, whether yesterday or a year ago, but towards *all* values without exception, including the ones that are guiding one's actions right now. An athlete who, at the very moment when he is breathless while concentrating on winning, ranks rest equally with winning, pleasure with eating well, work well done, friendship, or any other possible object of desire, and then compares these diverse objects impartially, well, then, *he* would be the picture of detachment. That would be a miracle.

One sees quite well by that illustration that philosophy does not consist in accumulating knowledge, as science does, but in changing the whole soul. Value is something that has a relation not only to knowledge but also to sensibility and action; there isn't any philosophical reflection without an essential transformation in sensibility and in the practices of life, a transformation that has an equal bearing on how one sees the most ordinary of circumstances and also the most tragic ones of life. Since value is nothing but an orientation of the soul, posing a value to oneself and being oriented towards it are one and the same thing; if one thinks at the same time two values that might pull one in two different directions, one will be oriented above all towards the value to which one awards the higher rank. Reflection supposes a transformation in the orientation of the soul that we call detachment. It has for its object establishing an order in the hierarchy of values, thus again a new orientation of the soul. Detachment is a renunciation of all possible ends without exception, a renunciation that puts a void in the place of the future just as the imminent approach of death does. This is why in the ancient mysteries, in Platonism, in the Sanskrit scriptures, in the Christian religion, and very probably everywhere and at every time, detachment has always been compared to death, and the initiation into wisdom has been regarded as a sort of passage towards death.

The assertion that philosophical reflection is infallible is absolutely contrary to common opinion; generally, it is thought that there are only conjectures in philosophy. What motivates this opinion are the contradictions between philosophical systems and the ones on the inside of each system. People believe that every philosopher has a system that contradicts all the others!—but, actually, far from being the case, there is a tradition, genuinely philosophical, that is as old as humanity itself, and that, we hope, will last as long. This tradition does not inspire, as from a common spring, *everyone* who is a philosopher, but very many are inspired by it. These are philosophers who may be different from each other in numerous ways but whose thoughts are nearly equivalent. Plato is the most perfect representative of this tradition; the *Bhagavad-Gita* is similarly inspired, and one should find easily Egyptian and Chinese texts named alongside them. In Europe, in modern times, it is necessary to cite Descartes and Kant; among recent thinkers, Lagneau and Alain in France, Husserl in Germany. This philosophical tradition, that is what we call philosophy. Although one could reproach it for its variations, it is one, eternal, and not susceptible of progress. The only renewal of which it is capable is that of expression, as when a man expresses himself to himself but still has to speak as he would to the people around him, in terms drawn from the conditions of his age, or his civilization, or the place where he lives.

It is desirable that such a transposition be done from one age to another, and it is the only reason why there is any value in going to the effort of writing on a subject after Plato has written on it.

The profound identity of these philosophers is hidden by the apparent differences that come from difficulties of vocabulary. Language isn't made to express philosophical reflection. Reflection can only use language by an adaptation of words that transforms their sense, without their new signification itself being able to be defined by words. This signification only appears by looking at the ensemble of formulas by which an author expresses his thought. It is therefore necessary not only to know all these formulas but to have a sense of them as a whole, and to consider them from the same point of view as the author—to be able to place oneself at the center of the thought of the author. It is the same with philosophical work as it is with certain pictures: they are only a heap of colors until one looks at them from a certain vantage point where they are all ordered. Thus to compare the assertions of different authors doesn't make any sense. If one wants to compare them, it is necessary to put oneself at the center of each one's thought and then to give an account as to whether their works proceed from the same mind. Now, a philosopher will hardly make this effort with regard to his predecessors, and as a consequence will not know whether he offers a parallel to them or not. But whether he knows it or not hardly matters.

It is true that there are authors who are not inspired by this tradition; that is not surprising, since philosophical reflection implies detachment and detachment is a sort of miracle. Many authors who believe themselves to be philosophers, and are believed to be such, are incapable of reflection, in the rigorous sense of the word, or are not capable of it in a sustained manner so that one could say that their work is inspired by it. Nevertheless, among these authors, some of them are of the first order, and their works merit the greatest interest. Moreover, there are authors who practice reflection and are not continually inspired by it and at all points. Their thought has weaknesses, and these weaknesses can sometimes cause divergences between them and other thinkers of the same race.

With respect to contradictions, all philosophical thought contains them. Far from being an imperfection of philosophical thought, it is an essential characteristic of it without which there would only be the false appearance of philosophy.

For true philosophy does not construct anything. Its object is given, namely, our thoughts. It only makes an inventory of them, as Plato said. If in the course of making this inventory it finds contradictions, the inventory does not depend on philosophy to suppress them, for then it would lie. Philosophers who attempt to construct systems in order to eliminate these contradictions are those who justify the appearance that lets people think that philosophy is something conjectural. For such systems can be varied infinitely, and there is no reason to have to choose one over another. But from the point of view of knowledge, these systems are below even the level of conjecture, for conjectures are at least inferior thoughts, and these systems are not thoughts. One cannot think them. One cannot, because if one did, even for an instant, one would eliminate during this second the contradictions at stake, and one cannot eliminate them. The contradictions that reflection finds in thought when it makes an inventory of it are essential to thought. They are present to their thought even during the time when thinkers are elaborating or exposing their system, it is just that they are using words in a special sense that doesn't conform to what they are thinking. This comes from an excessive ambition. Thus those who deny the reality of the exterior world, at the moment that they say they deny it, have the sense of the reality of their table and chair as any peasant does. They distinguish between their perceptions and their dreams just as any peasant does. In order to take an example that is clearer, saying that a line has a discrete length and at the same time contains an infinite number of points implies a contradiction; it is thinking the same thing as both finite and infinite. But the Greeks who said that a line is composed of a finite number of points were only pushed to do so by the desire of eliminating this contradiction; they didn't think what they were saying, because one can't think it. One cannot think *parts* of lines, repeated in the line a finite number of times, other than as definite lengths, and thus one cannot think them as being indivisible, for no matter how small you make them, you can still divide them further. The contradiction that one wants to eliminate reappears; it is better to expose it from the beginning. We make decisive progress if we decide to expose honestly the contradictions essential to thought instead of vainly trying to brush them aside. Doing that would mean that a large number of formulas devoid of sense would disappear from philosophy, but also from the sciences, making them more precise, not less. With respect to the completed systems constructed with the intention of eliminating all the essential contradictions of thought, we see that they do have value, but only as poetry.

This is exactly what Valéry was trying to say.

NOTE

1. There is a fragment of the manuscript missing here. (Ed.)

CHAPTER THREE

Philosophy

(*La philosophie*)

Throughout her life, Weil frequently wrote journalistic reports such as this one, which was published in *Cahiers du Sud* in May 1941. Most of them were political in nature; this philosophical review is therefore somewhat unusual and was in good part due to her ongoing connection with *Cahiers du Sud* while in Marseille. The specific occasions for this philosophical report were two lectures given in Marseille at the Society of Philosophical Studies, and Gaston Berger's dissertation defense. It is largely a report on the words of others, but Weil's own thinking about the nature of philosophy comes through very clearly, perhaps even more clearly than the words of others. Thus this report not only hints at but even replays many of Weil's own themes on the nature of philosophy and value. A chief example comes when at the end she spells out the distinction she makes in "Reflections on the Concept of Value" between the genuine philosopher and the one who is a poet, a mere system builder.

Lovers of philosophy in Marseille had three occasions to meet over the last few weeks. The Society of Philosophical Studies ended its series of lectures by invoking the two sources of wisdom and serenity, the Orient and Greece, towards which the present distressing situation is now pushing so many minds. And the president of this Society, Gaston Berger, defended his thesis at Aix-en-Provence.

M. Marcel Brion, who is known for his work in aesthetics, among other subjects, undertook a highly interesting investigation of the relation between painting and philosophy in China. This, of course, dealt with Taoism. Rightly, he only mentioned Confucius in passing; the marvelous texts that he cited were entirely drawn from Taoist writings and Buddhist writings near to Taoism. Listening to them, one soon sensed that claiming a relation between philosophy and painting was nothing forced, for these texts have a clear relation to artistic meditation. Unfortunately, the limited time of a lecture hardly lets one be as precise about the relation as one would like, and M. Brion had to stop at the very moment that his audience wanted him to say more, for he had just gotten to the heart of his subject. At least he left them wanting to spend some hours of contemplation before Chinese paintings. Or, not being able to do that, they could meditate on the Taoist formulas.

M. Brion spoke of how to get the interest and sympathy of those who continually compare the East unfavorably to the West. Certainly, whenever one makes the East one's subject, it is a good idea to compare it to the West only when one wants to do so in favor of the East, but perhaps it is too much to even insist on any opposition between the two. What is foreign to us in this thought? If we paid attention to it, we should recognize it as being something that is already present to us. Each Taoist formula strikes a chord in us, and these texts evoke one by one Heraclitus, Protagoras, Plato, the Cynics, the Stoics, Christianity, Jean-Jacques Rousseau. Not that Taoist thought is not original, profound, or new to a European; but, like all that is truly great, it is both new and familiar; we remember it, as Plato said, by having known it on the other side of the sky. This country that is on the other side of the sky, which Plato remembered, isn't it the same country as the one where, according to one of the texts cited by M. Brion, the wise man plays beyond the Four Seas and beyond space?

One can say just as much about art. A "painter-philosopher" is not a new idea for us, if we have ever read Leonardo da Vinci. If Leonardo was unique among us for saying that painting is philosophy that uses lines and color, he was not likely unique in thinking it. Isn't true art a method for establishing a certain relation between the world and the self, and between oneself and others, and isn't that the equivalent of philosophy? To be sure, many artists in the West have thought about it differently, but these are not the great ones. The great ones have without doubt thought about the relation as the painter did in a marvelous anecdote cited by M. Brion: having vainly invited the emperor to enter the grotto at the bottom of his painting, he went in alone and never returned. One can well imagine Giotto also walking into one of his frescos in Padua. When M. Brion spoke of the importance of empty space in Chinese painting—"Thirty spokes may come together at the hub, but it is the opening at the center that makes the wheel work," according to Lao-Tse—one thought also of Giotto, who used empty space to center his paintings to such powerful effect. The Chinese rejected the symmetry we have a taste for because, according to M. Brion, they chose the tree as their model of equilibrium, whereas we, following the Greeks, take the human being as our model; still, the common search for equilibrium in both makes them more alike than not. Chinese painters, according to M. Brion, had such a need for the infinite that they pushed perspective in a singular way and nearly dissolved forms; the Greeks looked for the definite, the limited, above all; this, however, is a human need. Man cannot be consoled by the infinite because it is not given to him; he tends to construct an infinite out of the finite; a construction that is probably the very definition of art. But if M. Brion, while presenting Chinese art to us as foreign, made it appear so near to us, well, that is the best tribute to his lecture.

M. Cornil, Dean of the Faculty of Medicine, by speaking to us of Hippocrates took us to the most beautiful age of Greece. He was highly qualified to do this, insofar as a doctor he both thinks about medicine and beyond it, and there is more merit to such a contemporary doctor than to an ancient one, since our culture locks everybody, nearly by force, into a specialty. M. Cornil did not make Hippocrates appear at all distant, an easy enough task when one knows and understands him. What, after all, is closer to us than Greece? It is nearer to us than we are to ourselves. It is doubtful that we have a single important idea that wasn't already clearly conceived by the Greeks, and M. Cornil recalled to us, for example, that they had clearly conceived of transformism.

Hippocrates had the concept of the experimental method as clearly, if not more so, than anybody in the following centuries. This was shown by the beautiful quotation chosen by M. Cornil with a surety of judgment worthy of a parallel subject: "I praise reasoning whenever it applies itself to experience and methodically links phenomena. If it takes as its point of departure facts as they evidently succeed each other, it will find the truth by the power of the meditation that insists on each particular object and then classifies all of them in their natural order of succession . . . I believe that every art is constituted by the procedure of observing all the facts in particular and grouping them analogically." M. Cornil threw a great deal of light on that in which Hippocrates' greatness consists: not in his attachment to experience, for in his time there were plenty of good empiricists, nor in his attachment to philosophy, for any number of philosophers delivered themselves on medicine, but in the methodical use of philosophical thought, in particular Pythagorean thought, to make a continual investigation of experience.

The Pythagorean method, as seen in Plato's *Philebus*, asks for theoretical reasons that in all studies of limited objects—which are by definition due to proportions, and are countable—are meant to classify the uncountable variety of particular cases. This method is still dominant today in science. The Hippocratic theory of "four humors" and the theory of critical days in an illness are applications of this method. Knowing that health and sickness are defined by relations, relations between the body and soul, between the parts of the body, humors, organs, functions, or between a human being and the environment and that there then is health when there is an equilibrium and harmony between them is a Pythagorean idea *par excellence*, and also a chief Hippocratic principle. It is an idea that we are far from exhausting. We can even understand it better today than we could fifty years ago, since the concept of wholism has reappeared in science—in biology and medicine, where Hippocrates' honor has been restored, and in physics, where people are starting to conceive of the study of phenomena taken as a whole, and in mathematics, where people are now standing on the base of theories of wholes and groups. But this evolution of science has hardly produced anything but trouble and disarray. What is missing is the virtue and intelligence needed to elevate us to the level of Greece, where thought was unified.

In a sense, Greek science is closer to our science than we might believe, as everything else is but a sketch of it. The *Epinomis* defines geometry as the knowledge of generalized number; Greek astronomers thought that the world was round and that the planets and the earth moved around the sun. Eudoxus, the inventor of the integral calculus, was able to conceive how to combine several movements in a single trajectory; Archimedes founded mechanics on the theory of the lever and physics, too, while searching for something analogous to the lever in natural phenomena. But in another sense, Greek science is far from us, far *above*, for the interrelation of its branches is apparent in all of the branches of science, and it is apparent in all forms of thought.

For the Greeks, epic poetry, drama, architecture, sculpture, their conception of the universe and of natural laws, astronomy, mechanics, physics, politics, the idea of virtue, each of these things bears at its center the concept of equilibrium that accompanies the concept of equilibrium, the soul of geometry. With this concept of equilibrium, which we have lost, they created science, our science. In their eyes, disequilibrium was only conceivable in relation to equilibrium, as a rupture of equilibrium. Illness, for example, was a problem with health. We, on the contrary, are inclined to think of health as a particular case of illness as it were, a limiting case, and that is a way of thinking that, extended to psychology, means, for many thinkers, starting with the baseness of the soul that is so widespread in our time. In Greece, the notion of equilibrium oriented all scientific investigations towards the Good, and medicine, as it was well understood, more than any other. M. Cornil showed through numerous quotes that in Hippocrates' eyes virtue and all forms of health were included in the definition of true medicine.

There can't be any question of our returning to Greece, for our country has never been in contact with Greek civilization, except perhaps during the time of Vercingetorix. But Vercingetorix was conquered, and the Druids, who perhaps had taught doctrines that were analogous to Pythagorean ones, were massacred by the Emperor Claudius. Still, if it were worth it to us, we could go towards Greece. A lecture such as that of M. Cornil can contribute to instilling that desire.

We were also transported to Greece by the thesis defense of M. Berger. Not that there was a specific question about Greece in the thesis itself; the complementary thesis dealt with the great German philosopher Husserl, but the primary thesis was an original work of Berger on the conditions of knowledge. But in the ensuing discussion—a task that the exceptionally clear mind of Berger made easy, even if one hadn't read the book in question—Plato was necessarily evoked. Berger's method, which consists, when one deals with an idea in mind, not in asking if it is true or false, but what it means, is the same as Socrates' method: "If we were clever, we would struggle the way the sophists do, opposing declarations to declarations; but we, simple men that we are, we want above all to consider in themselves, by themselves, what those things are that we are thinking." This is also the method of all the philosophers who belong to the Platonic tradition, such as Descartes or Kant. However, they have never formulated it, and have not given a clear enough account of it, which has hurt them. Truly said, there are only two kinds of philosophers, those who use this method and those who construct a representation of the universe according to their own taste. It is these latter philosophers alone who can be said to have "systems" whose value consists only in a certain poetic beauty and in the various marvelously penetrating individual formulas that are strewn throughout them, as is the case with Aristotle and Hegel. But the first sort of philosophers are the true masters of thought, and it is good to follow in their footsteps, as M. Berger does. His method allows him to eliminate insignificant problems. He refuses, for example, to pose the question of the value of knowledge, since knowledge is a given that is mixed with thought and that no thinking being can get away from. He also refuses to pose the problem of the existence of objects, because any existent foreign to us is given in our time, and is not any less exceptional, and we continually experience it. That is an excellent point of departure.

It is a singular thing that the philosophers who follow this method are all oriented towards salvation; M. Berger is no exception. It was pointed out, as if it were an original view, that he makes detachment a condition for philosophical reflection and that it is incumbent upon everybody; but, that is pure Plato: "It is necessary to turn towards the truth with the whole soul." For the rest, given this point, it is original, but he thinks simply as Plato did, and gives an account that Plato gave twenty-five hundred years ago; philosophy is to turn one towards the truth with all one's soul.

To be sure, we cannot give any further account here on whether or not the concepts and comparisons individually bear the imprint of a soul entirely turned towards the truth without having read and examined more closely Berger's book. In any case, M. Berger is perfectly capable of defending himself, without having to fear putting his thought clearly against any objections, which didn't seem very pertinent anyhow. For example, one member of his committee believed that he saw the book betraying a tendency to mysticism and an attraction towards Hindu thought—as if there were heresies in philosophy! Without doubt, Oriental mysticism often covers up some bad merchandise in the West, but that isn't its fault. If in philosophy one were to push aside the thoughts that seek to conceive what we call the transcendental, then it would be necessary to admit to philosophy only those that Plato called "the *un-initiated.*" Fortunately, we aren't there yet in our universities, because M. Berger did get his doctorate *magna cum laude.* And, something that is also comforting is that a number of students followed the discussion with attention, here in the city of Aix, with its yellow stones, its delicious nooks, and the young people filling the streets, all of which makes one think of an Italian university in the Renaissance.

CHAPTER FOUR

God in Plato

(Dieu dans Platon)

These pages were written in the early months of 1942. They were not intended as an essay and may well have been notes for a series of lectures convened by Father Perrin. They have a fragmentary aspect and do not seem to have been written continuously. In fact, as the editors of the *Oeuvres complètes* have suggested, it appears that in the beginning of these notes, Weil is not clear on the direction she wants to take with her subject matter, starting out with the observation that each people in antiquity had a spiritual vocation, but then focusing on the Greeks generally. However, she soon begins to concentrate on Plato, and the text becomes a series of translated texts of Plato with a running commentary on them. Moreover, there are numerous comments on her own comments, with many marginal and interlinear notes inserted. In order to help the reader get some sense of these layers, what is text and what are asides and hints for future direction, comments made in the margins and at the head and bottom of pages are indicated with "++" at their beginning and end; interlinear insertions are indicated similarly by a "<< ... >>."

++ Spirituality in Plato. That is, Greek spirituality. In Greece, Aristotle is perhaps the only *philosopher* in the modern sense, and he is entirely outside the Greek tradition—Plato is all that we have of Greek spirituality, and we have chiefly his popular works.

It is necessary to intuit. From the fact that an idea cannot be found in him, or not explicitly—So what is Plato? A *mystic* who has inherited a mystical tradition in which all of Greece was bathed. ++

Each ancient people had a vocation—except the Romans: an aspect of divine things. Israel: the unity of God. India: assimilation of the soul to God in mystical union. China: the way that God himself operates, the plentitude of action that seems to be inaction, the fullness of presence that seems to be absence, the void and silence. Egypt: immortality, the salvation of the just soul after death, by assimilation to a suffering God, dead and come to life, charity towards neighbor. Greece—(which had been influenced by Egypt)—: the misery of human beings, the distance, and the transcendence of God.

Greek history began with an atrocious crime, the destruction of Troy. Far from glorifying this crime as nations ordinarily do, the memory of it haunted the Greeks with remorse. They drew from it their sense of human misery. No people has expressed as they did the bitterness of human misery.

Iliad 24.527–33
>   In front of Zeus are placed two jars,
>   Where the gifts that he gives are, one good, the other evil.
>   Those for whom Zeus the hurler of thunder mixes his gifts,
>   Are sometimes afflicted; sometimes they prosper.
>   The one he gives gifts of disaster, he exposes to insults,
>   Awful need chases him across the divine earth.
>   He wanders and never receives any consideration from gods or men.

There is no picture of human misery that is more pure, more bitter and more poignant than the *Iliad*. The contemplation of the truth of human misery implies a very high spirituality. All Greek civilization is a research for bridges to throw up between human misery and divine perfection. Their art, to which nothing is comparable, their poetry, their philosophy, the science that they invented (geometry, astronomy, mechanics, physics, biology) were nothing but these bridges. They invented the idea of *mediation*.

But we have hardly any trace of Greek spirituality before the works of Plato. However, here are some fragments. An Orphic fragment:

You will find near the house of the dead, on the left, a spring.
Near it rises a white cypress.
Do not go towards this spring, nor approach it.
You will find another one, which flows from the lake of Memory.
Cold, rushing water. Before it are guards.
Tell them: I am the daughter of the Earth and the starry Heaven.
But my origin is celestial. That much, you yourselves know.
But thirst consumes and kills me. Ah! give me quickly that cold
    water that rushes from the lake of Memory.
And they will let you drink from that divine spring.
And then, with the other heroes, you will reign.

This text already contains a part of the Greek spirituality as we find it in Plato. It holds several things: First, that we are children of Heaven, that is to say, of God. That earthly life is a forgetting. Here below we have forgotten transcendent truth and the supernatural. Then, that the condition of salvation is thirst. It is necessary to thirst for the forgotten truth even to the point of feeling that this thirst is killing us. Finally, that this thirst is surely slaked. If we sufficiently thirst for this water, and if we know that it is ours to drink it insofar as we are children of God, it will be granted to us.

<< Fragments of Heraclitus: — Λόγος — Zeus — eternal fire. Fragment of Cleanthes. >>

Pythagoreans — center of Greek civilization. We know nearly nothing about them except through Plato.

Plato. There are two things to know about him:

1st. He is not a man who has invented a philosophical doctrine. Contrary to all other philosophers (without exception, I believe), he constantly repeats that he has invented nothing, that he is only following a tradition, one that he sometimes names and sometimes not. It is necessary to take him at his word.

He is sometimes inspired by earlier philosophers of whom we possess only fragments and whose systems he has assimilated into a superior synthesis, sometimes from his teacher, Socrates, and sometimes secret Greek traditions that we know little about, except from him, such as the Orphic tradition, the tradition of the Eleusinian mysteries, and very probably the traditions of Egypt and other Oriental countries.

<< We do not know if Plato was the very best in Greek spirituality: nothing else has come down to us. Pythagoras and his disciples were without doubt even more marvelous. >>

2nd. We only possess from Plato his popular works destined for the larger public. One can compare them to the parables of the Gospels. Just because an idea is not found in them, even implicitly, nothing permits us to think that Plato and the other Greeks did not have it.

It is necessary to penetrate to the interior by dwelling on indications that are sometimes very brief, and by bringing together scattered texts.

My interpretation: Plato is an authentic mystic, and even the father of Western mysticism.

Texts on God:
(The remarks on Θεοί, Θεός, ὁ Θεός.) ++ When he says Θεοί—is he making a joke?—Or, perhaps: divinity itself (cf. Elohim). Or perhaps it is often something analogous to the angels: finite beings, but perfectly pure. ++

Theaetetus 176

THEODORUS: Socrates, if you persuade the whole world as well as me, there would be more peace and less evil among men.

SOCRATES: But it is not possible that evil should ever disappear, Theodorus. For it is necessary that there always be something that is more or less contrary to the good (ὑπεναντίον). And this thing cannot have its place among the gods; but it is necessary that it circulate in the realm of mortal nature, in this world. This is why it is necessary to be forced to flee from here below as fast as one can. This flight from the world is *assimilation* to God in the measure to which that is possible. This assimilation consists in becoming just and holy with the help of reason. But, my dear man, it is not easy to persuade men that it is necessary to flee from sin and to seek virtue for any other motive than the one that is common to human beings, who do not want to appear to be bad people, who want to appear virtuous. That is the foolishness of an old woman, I believe. The right reason is this one: *Never, in any way, is God unjust.* He is just to the supreme degree, and there is nothing more like him than the one who among us is the most just. Knowing that is wisdom and true virtue. To be ignorant of it is to be manifestly stupid and vile.

The other apparent habits, the other forms of wisdom that deal with politics, power, technique, are crude and mercenary. With respect to those who commit injustices, whose words or actions are impious, it is far better not to admit that they might be clever in their malice. For them a reproach is a cause for exulting, and they believe that they are being looked at as men who are not empty, useless weights upon the earth, but as real men, the kind everybody needs in order to remain safe and sound in a city. It is necessary to tell the truth, and to know that they are completely different from what they say they are. For they ignore the punishment of injustice; and this is the one thing in the world that one ought to ignore least. It is not what they think it is, such as death or a beating, things that unjust men do not submit to, but another sort of punishment that it is impossible to escape . . . There are in reality two models, the one divine and blessed, the other deprived of God and miserable. They do not see that it is that way. Their stupidity, their extreme ignorance hides from them that, in fact, in their unjust actions they are more like the second than the first, from which they differ. They are punished by the belief that they are living a life that accords with the model that they resemble.

Principal ideas: *flight* (violence of fear, June 1940). *Assimilation* (cf. Geometry—*Epinomis*): *God is perfectly just.* ++ The Greeks were *obsessed* by the idea of justice (because of Troy?) They died from having abandoned it. ++

There are two moralities. One is external, and is human; the other, the true one, is supernatural and comes from God and is merged with the knowledge (γνῶσις, a Gospel term) of the highest truth—[Remark on the four virtues.] The reward of the good consists in the faith that one is good, the punishment of the evil is in the fact that one is evil, and each is an automatic reward or punishment ("I do not judge, they condemn themselves.").

++ A very important consequence of this "assimilation." The *ideas* of Plato are the thoughts of God or God's attributes. ++

Said otherwise: Whereas in the domain of nature (which includes the psychological) good and evil are co-produced without end, but in the spiritual domain evil only produces evil and good only produces good. (The gospel.) And good and evil consist in the contact with (a contact of similarity) or the separation from God—(It is a question therefore of something quite different than an abstract conception of God that the human intelligence can arrive at without grace, it is an experimental conception.).

How is the imitation of God by a human being possible? We have one answer. It is Christ. What is Plato's response? Read here his passage on the perfectly just man.—We will discover this image of nudity again as it is linked to death in the *Gorgias*.

What is this justice?

Gorgias 523a–525a

Listen to a very beautiful story. You may think that it is a fable, but I think that it tells the truth. So what I am going to tell you I am telling you as the truth.

[It used to be that] final judgment was exercised by living people on living people; each was judged the day when he was about to die. This is why the judgments were bad. Pluto and the guardians of the Isles of the Blessed came to tell Zeus that men were going to shores that they did not deserve to go to. So Zeus said: "I will indeed put a stop to that. Bad judgments are being rendered at the present. That is because those who are being judged are judged while dressed, since they are being judged while alive. Too many criminal souls are dressed in beautiful bodies, noble and rich ones, and when the judgment takes place, too many of the witnesses who accompany them do so to witness to their having lived justly. All that makes an impression on the judges. Moreover, the judges are dressed, too. Their eyes, their ears, their body is a veil in front of their soul. All that is put before them, their own clothes and the clothes of the accused. So, first of all, it is therefore necessary that men no longer know ahead of time the hour of their death, for at the present they know it. Tell Prometheus that he is to put an end to that. Then it is necessary that they be naked at the time of judgment, all of them; it is necessary therefore that they be judged when dead. The judge also has to be naked, and he has to be dead; with his own soul he needs to contemplate the soul itself of each one as soon as he has died, abandoned by all his neighbors and having left on earth all his adornment here below, all so that his judgment may be just. For myself, knowing these things before us, I have chosen my sons as judges [. . .] and when they have died they will judge in the meadow at the crossroads from where the two routes leave, one to the Isles of the Blessed, and the other to Tartarus.

Death in my eyes is nothing but the separation of two things, the soul and the body; and when they are separated, each is pretty nearly in the same state as when the man was living . . . If someone . . . had a big body . . . then his corpse will be big . . . and so on for the rest. If he had while he was alive traces of the blows of a whip, or of scars from beatings and wounds, all that will be seen on his body when it is dead. It seems to me that it is the same with the soul. Everything in the soul becomes apparent when it is naked and stripped of the body, all its natural dispositions and the effects on it of every one of its attachments to things. When we arrive before the judge . . . he will contemplate the soul of each of us without knowing to whom it belongs, but often, seizing that of the Great King or of another king or of another powerful man, he sees that because of their lies and injustices that the soul is filled with the blows of whips and with scars that were impressed on it by each of its actions, that all is twisted by the effects of lying and vanity, that nothing is right with it because it has been raised without truth.[. . .]

Believe me therefore and follow me into this place that assures us when we get there of a happy life and a happy death. And let anybody despise you as an idiot, and insult you, if he wants, and, by Zeus, put up with the shame of that slap in the face of which you speak so often; for you will not suffer anything so very terrible by it if you are truly good and beautiful, well disciplined in virtue.

We find in this text:

1st. Again the idea that judgment is nothing other than the expression of what each person is in reality. Not an appreciation of what he has done, but the affirmation of what he is. Bad actions are only counted in the scars that they leave on the soul. There is nothing arbitrary in this; it is a rigorous necessity.

2nd. The image of nakedness linked to death. This double image is a mystical one par excellence.

There is no one so wise, so all seeing, so just that he may not be influenced by the physical aspects of people and even more so by their social situations. ("if you suppose . . .") The effects of the imagination. No one is insensible to clothes. Victory or defeat, etc.

The truth is hidden by all these things. THE TRUTH IS SECRET. ("Your father who is in secret . . .") The truth is manifest only in naked-ness, and *nakedness is death, which is to say, the rending of all the at-tachments that constitute for each human being their reason for living*, neighbors, the opinion of others, material possessions and morals, everything.

Plato does not say, but he does imply, that in order to become just, which requires self-knowledge, that it is necessary to become naked and dead already in this life. The examination of conscience demands this rupture of all the attachments that constitute our reasons for living.

Moreover, he says explicitly in the *Phaedo* (64a–67d):

Those who are properly dedicated to the search for wisdom do not practice anything other than dying and being dead . . . Death is nothing other than the fact that the soul is separated from the body . . . The soul of the person who seeks wisdom hates the body and flees far from it and seeks to be alone with itself . . . If we want to understand purely what something is, we should separate our-selves from the body and contemplate things with the soul itself. . . . It is at this moment only, it seems to me, that we will possess what we desire, what we call ourselves lovers of, namely, reason; this is to say after our death, not while we are still alive. For if it is impos-sible with the body to understand anything purely, then either we will never know, or we will know only after death; for then the soul will be in itself, by itself, and far from the body, but not before then. And insofar as we are alive, it seems that we will be much closer to knowing when we have neither commerce nor union with the body beyond what is strictly necessary; then we will not be overwhelmed by its nature, and then we will purify ourselves from it as far as God himself delivers us . . . Purification consists in separating to the greatest extent possible the soul from the body, training it, and training it alone by itself without any contact with the body, to get it used to collecting and recollecting to the highest degree, now and in the future, alone by itself and as liberated from any attachments to things. Now, the detachment and separation of the soul from its relation to the body is what we call death.

It is nearly certain that this double image of nakedness and death as a symbol of salvation comes from the traditions of those secret cults that the ancients called the mysteries. Babylonian text of Ishtar in hell. Seven doors. At each one, we have to give up something.

++ The meaning of this image of the door: knock and it will be opened to you. ++ Osiris, and of course Dionysios, die and come to life—Descent into hell as an initiation.

Role of this double image in Christian spirituality. Death, St. Paul. Nakedness, St. John of the Cross, St. Francis.

If justice demands that during this life one be naked and dead, it is clear that this is something impossible for human nature, and so supernatural.

That which above all keeps the soul from being assimilated to God by justice is the flesh, of which Plato says, following the Orphics and Pythagoreans: "The body is the soul's tomb."

Philolaos: "[We know] from the witness of the ancient theologians and prophets that the soul is chained to the body as a punishment and as it were buried in this tomb."

There are a number of texts of Plato on the perils of the flesh.

Plato also took another image from the Pythagoreans comparing the sensible and carnal part of the soul, the seat of desire, to a vat that is sometimes sound, and sometimes full of holes. According to them, whoever has not received the light, for that one the vat is leaky, and such people are continually occupied with trying to pour everything they can into it, but never succeed in filling it.

But a greater obstacle than the flesh is society. There is a terrible image of this. An idea of first importance in Plato that runs through all his works but is only given explicit expression in this passage, for reasons that the passage itself will explain. One cannot ever underestimate its importance.

Republic VI, 492a–493a

Do you believe, like the vulgar, that only a few adolescents are corrupted by the sophists, and that it is only a few particular sophists who do it, and that it is hardly worth talking about? Those who do talk about it are themselves the greatest sophists, for these are the ones who are in complete charge of education, modeling both young and old, men and women according to their desires—But when? he asked. When, Socrates said, a large crowd gets together in an assembly, or a tribunal, or a theater, or an army, or in any other place of massive get-togethers tumultuously blaming or praising with words or acts. They blame and praise to excess, they cry, they clap their hands, and the rocks themselves and the place where they are found echo and redouble the noise of blame and praise.

++ N.B. This seems particular to Athens, but it is necessary to transpose it. The following shows that Plato had in view all types of social life without exception. ++

In such circumstances, what is going to be the state of a young man's heart? What special education can make him resist and not be submerged by all these criticisms and elegies, not sweep him along in the flood? He will declare then things beautiful and things ugly in conformity to the view of others, he will attach himself to the same things as they do, he will become like them.—There would be a powerful compulsion, Socrates—And yet, Socrates said, I still have not spoken of the greatest one—Which?—The compulsion that these educators, these sophists exercise on those whom they do not persuade. Can you ignore the fact that those who do not allow themselves to be persuaded are punished by them with disgrace, or fines or death? Thus, do you believe that another sophist, that any arguments spoken by individuals can be raised against them with any success? No, the undertaking itself would be madness.
For there is not, and there never has been, and there never will be any other teaching of morality than that of the crowd [τούτων]. At least no other human teaching. For certainly it is always necessary to make an exception for what is divine. It is indeed necessary to know, that whoever is saved and has become what he ought to be in the middle of such a structure as society, that person, if we want to speak correctly, is saved by a predestination that comes from God. [Θεοῦ μοῖραν αὐτὸ λέγων οὐ κακῶς ἐρεῖς]

(N.B. It is impossible to state more categorically that grace is the unique source of salvation, that salvation comes from God and not from man. The allusions to tribunals, the theater, etc., which refer to Athenian institutions, might make one believe that this conception has no general import; but the words "there is not, and there never has been, and there never will be . . ." show the opposite. The crowd imposes itself under various different modes in all societies without exception. There are two moralities, social morality and supernatural morality, and only those who are enlightened by grace have access to the latter.)

++ The wisdom of Plato is not a philosophy, a search for God by means of human reason. Aristotle made such an effort and did it as well as anyone can. But the wisdom of Plato is nothing other than an orientation of the soul towards grace. ++

With respect to those individuals who give paid lessons, the crowd calls them sophists and regards them as rivals. But they do not teach anything other than the opinions of the crowd. This is what they call wisdom. Imagine a large and strong beast; its keeper learns what angers it and what it wants and how one needs to approach it, where one can touch it, at what times and then what causes it to be irritable or gentle, what cries it makes when it is in such and such a mood, what words might appease it and which annoy it. Imagine that having learned all that by experience, he then calls that knowledge wisdom. He even writes a textbook on it and gives a course on it. Among all these opinions and desires, he does not at all know in truth what is beautiful or ugly, good or bad, just or unjust. He applies all these terms to the various functions of the great beast. Whatever pleases the beast, he calls good; whatever it rejects he calls bad, and he has no other criterion for this subject. Things that are necessary he calls just and fine, for he is incapable of seeing or showing to anyone else that in reality there is a difference between the essence of the necessary and that of the good. Wouldn't this be a strange teacher? Well, this is exactly the person who thinks that it is the essence of wisdom to observe the pleasures and tastes of a gathered mob, whether it is in matters of painting, or music or politics. For if someone traffics with the herd and offers to it a poem or any other work of art or political conception, if he submits to the crowd anything beyond the domain of necessary things, a necessity as hard as bronze will make him do only what the crowd approves.

This great beast, which is the beast of sociality, is from all evidence the same as the beast of the *Apocalypse*.

This Platonic conception of society as an obstacle between man and God, an obstacle that God alone can cross over, can also be compared to these words of the devil to Christ in the Gospel of St. Luke:

He showed him in the space of an instant all the kingdoms on earth. And the devil said to him: "I will give you all the power and the glory that goes with these. For it has been left to me, to me and to whomever it pleases me to make a part of it. (4:5–6)

<< The saying of Richelieu. Machiavelli.—Marxism insofar as it is true. Irreducible evil that one can only try to limit. >>

It is difficult to grasp the import of this Platonic conception, because we do not know at what point one is a slave of social influences. By its very nature, slavery is nearly always unconscious, and at the moments when it is revealed to consciousness, there is always the help of lying to veil it from oneself.

Two remarks, to clarify things a bit:

1. The opinions of the great beast are not necessarily contrary to the truth. They are formed by accident. *It loves certain bad things and hates certain good ones; but on the other hand, there are good things that it loves and bad things that it hates.* But even when its opinions *conform to the truth they are still essentially alien to the truth.*

For example, if one is tempted to steal but holds off, there is a big difference between restraining oneself out of obedience to the great beast and doing so out of obedience to God.

The trouble is that one can very easily tell oneself that one is obeying God when one is really obeying the great beast. For words can always be used to serve no matter what master.

Thus, the fact is, if there is a point on which one thinks one is acting in conformity to the truth, that proves nothing about whether one is a slave of the great beast on this point or not.

++ All the virtues have a copy of themselves in the morality of the great beast, except humility. This is the key to the supernatural.

Thus it is mysterious, transcendent, indefinable, and unrepresentable. (Egypt) ++

2. In fact, all that contributes to our *education consists exclusively in things that at one time or another have been approved by the great beast.*

Racine, *Andromaque* and *Phèdre.* If he had begun with *Phèdre.*

History; the men whose names have come down to us became famous by the great beast. Those who did not turn out to be famous remain unknown to both their contemporaries and to posterity.

Finally, it should be noted that it was the disapproval of the great beast that led all of Christ's disciples to abandon him without exception. Since we are worth much less than they are, it is certain that the great beast has at least as much power over us, without our taking any account of the fact, and that is even worse; at all instants, at this moment now. And the part of us that it owns, God does not.

Parenthetically, such a theory of society implies that society is essentially evil (and on that Machiavelli was only a disciple of Plato, as was nearly everybody in the Renaissance), and that the reform or transformation of society cannot have any other reasonable object than making it as little evil as is possible. Plato understood this, and his construction of an ideal city in the *Republic* is purely symbolic. This is frequently misunderstood.

++ Rule: do not submit to society outside the domain of necessary things. ++

Having recognized, then, that grace coming from God is necessary, in what does it consist, by what process does it work, in what way does the human receive it? Texts; *Republic, Phaedrus, Symposium.* Plato makes use of images. The fundamental idea of these images is that the disposition of the soul that mentally receives these images and welcomes grace is nothing other than love. The love of God is the root and foundation of Plato's philosophy. *Republic.* Comparison between the good and the sun.

++ *Fundamental idea*; Love oriented towards its proper object, which is to say, perfection, puts it in contact with the only absolutely real reality. Protagoras said: "Man is the measure of all things." Plato replies: "Nothing imperfect is the measure of anything" and "God is the measure of all things." ++

(Note that the Sun was an image of God for the Egyptians; in Peru, before the Spanish discovered and destroyed this country, the Sun was adored as a unique divinity, and looked at as the symbol of God, whom they considered to be too elevated to be the object of direct worship.)

Republic VI, 505d–e
The good is what all soul seeks, it is why it acts; soul has a presentiment that it is something real, but is uncertain and is incapable of sufficiently grasping what it is; and it cannot on this point, as with other matters, have a firm belief. (Something more than a belief is needed.)

<< The good is above justice and the other virtues; we seek them out insofar as they are good. *Symposium* 205e–206a, *It is not true to say that a man cherishes his own. There is no other object of desire for human beings except the good.* >>

Socrates says that he is going to explain the good by an image —

Republic VI, 507b–509b
There are many beautiful things, good things and the like. But the beautiful itself, the good itself and so on, when we speak of them, we establish what each one of these things is according to a unique idea of a unique essence. We see things, but we do not conceive them (νοεῖσθαι). Ideas, however, we conceive but we do not see them. We see visible things by sight. But when there is both something to be seen and sight, something is still missing. Although the eye is capable of seeing and tries to make use of its sight, and there are objects that have color, still the eye will not see and the colors will not be seen if there is not a third thing tailored for vision, namely, light . . . The sun is not sight. It is not the organ of sight that we call the eye. But of all the organs of sense the eye is the one that is most like the sun.
You see what I called the offspring of the good, for the good has engendered something analogous to itself. For the good is in the spiritual (νοητός) world to the spirit (νοῦν) and to spiritual things (νοούμενα), what the sun in the visible world is to sight and to things that we see. When the eyes are not turned towards things whose colors are illumined by the light of day, but towards those

that are in a nocturnal light, they are dim and nearly blind, as if there were no sight in them. Every time that they are turned towards things that the sun shines on, they see clearly.

It is the same for the spiritual eye of the soul. Every time that it rests on something that is resplendent with truth and reality, it conceives (ἐνόησε), it knows and it is manifest that it is spirit. When it rests on that which is mixed with shadows, on what comes to be and perishes, it only has opinions, it is darkened, it mixes up its opinions, and it seems that it is not spirit.

That which is the source (παρέχον) of truth for things known and of the faculty of knowing for the being who knows, it is necessary to say that it is the idea of the good. It is necessary to think that it is the author (αἰτίαν) of both knowledge and the truth insofar as it is an object of knowledge. These are two beautiful things, knowledge and truth, but in order to think correctly one will have to think that the idea of the good is even more beautiful still. With reason one can look here below at light and vision as things that are kin to the sun, but are not the sun itself. In the same way one can with reason look at knowledge and truth as being things similar to the good, but that are not the good itself. That which constitutes the good is even more honored.

But it is necessary to consider once more the image of the good. The sun does not only give to visible things the ability to be seen, but it also makes them come to be, and their growth and nourishment, while it itself does not partake in becoming. In the same way, the good does not only give to things known the ability to be known. It is by the good that they exist. Their being comes from it, although the good is not being; for it exceeds being in dignity and truth.

Republic VI, 518b–d

Do not think that education is what some people claim that it is. For, they claim, that since knowledge is not in the soul, that they are going to put it there, as if they could put sight into blind eyes. Well, what we have demonstrated is that the faculty of learning and the organ of this faculty are found in the soul of each person. But it was seen to be there like an eye that could not turn away from shadows and turn itself towards the light other than by turning the whole body. Thus, it is necessary to turn oneself with one's whole soul away from things that change, until the soul has become capable of supporting the contemplation of being (of the real?) and that which is even more luminous in being,—to know, as we have said, the good. Thus the art that is needed here is the art of conversion, which shows the easiest way and the most effective way of making the soul turn. It is not a question of producing vision in it, for it is already capable of seeing, but it is not turned towards where it needs to look, and does not see aright, so it is turning above all that is needed.

[Instead of saying "being" perhaps this should be translated as: "reality" and "the real"?]

Some remarks.

VISION IS INTELLIGENCE, THE RIGHT ORIENTATION IS SUPERNATURAL LOVE.

Although Plato expresses himself in strictly impersonal terms, this good that is the author of intelligibility and being and truth is nothing other than God. Plato only uses the word "author" in order to indicate that God is a person. It is a matter of being a person.

Plato in giving to God the name of "the good" expresses as strongly as possible that God is, for a human being, where love is directed.

Republic VI, 505e

> *The good is what all soul seeks, it is why it acts; soul has a presentiment that it is something real, but it is uncertain and it is incapable of sufficiently grasping what it is.*

Cf. St. Augustine. God is a good that is nothing other than good. That is from Plato. *Symposium* 205e–206a: "It is not true to say that a man cherishes his own (not egoism). There is no other object of desire for human beings except the good."

Two ideas.

1. *There is not, there cannot be any other relation between a human and God except love. What is not love has no relation to God.*

2. The object belonging to love is God, and *everyone who loves anything other than God deceives oneself, and is in error, as if one were to run towards a stranger in the street as a result of mistaking him for a friend.*

It follows that it is only insofar as the soul is oriented towards what it is necessary to love, that is to say, insofar as it loves God, that it is fit to love and know. It is impossible for a man to exercise fully his intelligence *without charity*, because there is no other source of light than God. Thus the faculty of supernatural love is above the intelligence and is its condition. *The love of God is the unique source of all certitudes.*

<< (Plato's philosophy is nothing other than an act of love towards God.) >>

Being (reality) that proceeds from the good is not the material world, for that is not being, but a perpetual mixture of becoming and passing away, it is changing. Neither is being that proceeds from the good the conceptions that our intelligence has the capacity to manipulate and define. For, further on, Plato compares the most precise conceptions to shadows, and to the reflections and images of things in the water.

This being is transcendent in its relation to nature and to human intelligence. The light that is shed upon it is not of the same nature as the intelligibility found in the sciences that are within our reach. It, too, is a transcendent light.

Hence, it seems difficult not to regard this being as God, and this light as God. It seems difficult to interpret these three notions of the good, of truth, and of being other than as a conception of the *Trinity*.

Cf. *Parmenides* 143e. If the one is, there is the one, being, and the link between the two (and from that all numbers). But this is purely abstract. (If the one truly is one, it is not at all) — [We know from Aristotle that the One was one of the names that Plato gave to God.] —

(The Good corresponds to the Father, being to the Son, and truth to the Spirit.)

It is evident that Plato regards true wisdom as something supernatural. One cannot express more clearly than he does the opposition between the two possible conceptions of wisdom. Those who regard wisdom as a possible addition to human nature think that when someone becomes wise that a human effort has put into him something that was not there before, and that somebody, himself or somebody else, has put this thing in him.

Plato thinks that whoever has arrived at true wisdom has nothing more in himself than before, because wisdom is not in him, but is perpetually coming to him from somewhere else, namely, God.

++ What one person can do for another is not to add something to him, but to turn him towards the light that comes from elsewhere, from on high. ++

Nothing has been done to him except to have been turned towards the source of wisdom, to be converted.

This light that comes from the truth is, therefore, inspiration.

But although we can change where we look while leaving the body immobile or nearly so, it is not this way with the soul. The soul cannot look in another direction without being entirely turned.

The soul, in order to turn and look towards God, therefore has to be entirely turned away from things that are born and that perish, that change, and from temporal things (exact equivalence). The entire soul, and that includes, therefore, the part of it that senses, the carnal part of the soul that is rooted in sensible things and that draws its life from them. It has to be uprooted. This is death. Conversion is this *death*.

++ Intelligence resides in everyone. The use of the intelligence has supernatural love as its condition (this is not intellectualism, quite the contrary). ++

The loss of something or someone to which we are attached is immediately sensed by us by a weakening that corresponds to a loss of energy. *For it is necessary to lose all vital energy that is given to us by the totality of things and beings to which we are attached.* It is indeed therefore a death.

Thus total detachment is a condition of the love of God, and whenever the soul has made the move of detaching itself totally from this world in order to turn itself wholly towards God, it is enlightened by the truth that descends upon it from God.

This is the same notion that is at the center of Christian mysticism.

Note that it is the *whole* soul. Cf. St. John of the Cross. The least attachment prevents the transformation of the soul. *As coming short by a single degree of heat can keep wood from being lit* (cf. the Stoics); *as a thread ever so slight can keep a bird from flying, unless it is cut . . .* That is what Plato means by this little phrase: *all* the soul.

How does conversion work? And, above all, what is the human before conversion? The image of the cave. A terrible image of human misery. *We are that way* (not we were).

Republic VI, 514a–516c

Think of people having for their home an underground cavern that has an opening towards the light along its whole width—They have been in this cavern since infancy, and their legs and their necks are held in chains. Thus they have to remain motionless, and can only look at what is before them, and they cannot turn their heads because of the chains. The light comes to them from a fire that is burning above them, and quite far behind them. Between the fire and these chained creatures, and above them, there is walkway along which a screen has been built, like the barrier that puppeteers put between themselves and their audience, and from behind which they show their puppets. Imagine now some men who are moving along this walkway carrying all sorts of figures and lifting them as they go past the wall, figures of people and animals all of wood and stone and all sorts of manufactured objects. As people normally do, those who are carrying the figures sometimes talk and sometimes are silent.

This is a strange image, Glaucon said, and all these chained creatures are strange.

They are like us, said Socrates. And in your view, could these beings see anything else other than themselves and their neighbors, anything other than the shadows projected by the fire on the wall of the cavern that they face?

How could they see anything else, said Glaucon, since they are forcibly constrained and have to keep their heads fixed? And the same thing goes for the objects that are being carried. And if they were to speak about it, necessarily they would believe that in giving names to the things they see they are naming things that are really there. And if there was an echo in the cavern when one of those walking spoke, they would think that what is said belongs to the passing shadow. In a general way, such creatures would believe that there is nothing real except the shadows of artificial objects.

Think about, therefore, what their deliverance and healing from their chains and their madness might be, if in the course of nature they were discovered in such a state. When one of them was freed, when he was *forced* suddenly to stand up, to turn his head, to walk, to look towards the light, each of these actions would be painful and the dazzling brightness would keep him from seeing the objects that he had seen before as shadows . . .What would he say if someone came along and told him that before this what he had seen was only so much nonsense; that now he is nearer to reality, that having turned towards reality he is looking in a better direction? If in showing him each of the objects that had been passed before him, we asked him "what is this?" what would he have to answer? He could only know to say and think that what he had seen before was truer than what he was being shown now. And if one forced him to turn towards the light itself his eyes would hurt and he would flee and turn towards the things that he can see, and he would think that they are truly clearer than what we were showing him. And if one pulled him by force from that place, across the rough ascent and the escarpment, without letting him go until he had come to the light of the sun; that would be torture for him, and he would revolt against whoever was dragging him, and once they came to the light his eyes would be full of splendor, and he would not be able to see a single thing that we told him was true. He would have to get used to it before he could raise his eyes. At first, he would look more easily at shadows and then he could look at the reflections of human beings and other beings in the water, then at the beings themselves. Then, he would have little difficulty in contemplating the things of the sky and of the night sky, looking at the light of the moon and of the stars, and then the sun and its light in full day. But at the very end, *I think he could look at the sun full face, not its image in the water or other places, but the sun itself, in its own place, and as it really is.*

++ State of perfection. Cf. St. John: καθώς ἐστιν. ++

Then he would take account of the fact that it is the sun itself that produces the seasons and years, that rules all that is found in the visible world and that is in a certain way the cause of all that he sees. And if he remembers his first home, and the wisdom of the underground, and his companions in chains, would he account them happy, would not he take them [to be pitied and consider himself happy in the change]?

[According to the little that we know of the mysteries, it is very probably that this image is taken from their traditions and that perhaps even a time underground in chains constituted a rite for them.]

Cf. *The Hymn to Demeter*

One cannot push a portrayal of human misery further than this.

We were born punished. Pythagorean idea. It is not a question of an original fault, but such a fault is implied insofar as this description has a penal color to it, the color of prison.

We are born and live *in a lie*. Lies only are given to us. Even ourselves; we believe we see ourselves, and we see only the shadow of ourselves. "Know yourself": this is an unpracticable precept in the cave. We only see the shadow of the artificial. This world where we are and of which we see only shadows (appearances) is an artificial thing, a game, a simulacrum. A contrast to consider deeply. Being that is truly being, the intelligible world, is *produced* by the supreme Good, it emanates from it. The material world is *fabricated*.

It is impossible to put a greater distance between our universe and God.

(The material world, let it be said in passing, is *in* the intelligible world, which is infinitely more vast. One cannot be farther than Plato is from pantheism, of putting God into the world.)

We are born and we live *in passivity*. We do not budge. Images pass before us and we live them. We choose nothing. What we live, at each instant, is what is given to us by the puppet master. (No one has said anything to us about him . . . Prince of this world?) We have absolutely no liberty. One is free after conversion (and even during it) but not before. As Maine de Biran said, we are modified.

Movie theaters are quite similar to the cave. That shows how much we love our degradation.

We are born and live *in unconsciousness*. We are unconscious of our misery. We do not know that we are under punishment, that we dwell in falsity, that we are passive, nor, indeed, do we know that we are unconscious. If the story of the cave were literally true, this is exactly what would be its result. This is always the effect of the degradation of affliction: the soul, that the soul sticks to it until it can no longer detach itself.

++ Ersatz of resignation. ++

And this is the effect of the general affliction that is common to all of us in that we are human beings.

If the shadows passing along the wall have frightening shapes, the chained captives suffer because of them. But the captives have not the faintest idea of the real essence of their misery, which is their total dependence on the passing shadows and the error that makes them believe that these shadows are real.

Hence conversion is no small thing. Still, the disappearance of the chains is only half of it.

One can imagine that the chains fall off when a human being has received by inspiration, or more often by being instructed by another, orally or by the written word (often it is a book), the idea that this world is not everything, that there is something better and it is necessary to seek it out.

But when one begins to budge, inertia and stiffness hinder us, and the least movement is intolerably painful. The comparison here is of a marvelous precision.

There is one way of making things very easy. If the one who has made the chains fall away has told of the marvels of the outside world, of plants, trees, the sky, the sun, we only have to stay still, close our eyes, and imagine that we are leaving, that we are climbing out of the cave and that we are looking at all those things. In order to make the imagination even more vivid, we can also imagine that we are experiencing some of the sufferings attached to this journey.

This procedure gives us a very agreeable life, with all the great satisfactions of self-love, and all of it without costing us anything.

Anytime that one thinks that a conversion took place without a certain minimum quantity of violence and pain, well, that conversion never truly took place. The chains have fallen, but the creature has remained immobile and has only budged fictively—

<< But what is the criterion? The sense of effort and of suffering are not it; there are imaginary sufferings and efforts. There is no greater deceiver than the inner sense. There has to be another criterion. >>

Plato's image indicates that conversion is a violent and painful operation, a tearing away, and carries with it an irreducible quantity of violence and pain that it is impossible to cut out of the process.

<< If one cannot pay the whole price, one will not get to the goal, even if one has cut out very little >>

In everything that is real there is something irreducible.

Plato's comparison indicates the steps in this operation.

The captive whose chains have dropped off walks across the cave. He can make nothing out; moreover, he truly is in the twilight. It would not be of any help for him to stop and examine his surroundings. It is necessary that he walk, whatever might be the price of a thousand pains and not knowing where he is going. The will here alone moves him; the intelligence plays no role. It is necessary to make a new effort in each step, and if he stops trying before he gets out, even if he is short by a single step, he will not get out. The last steps are the hardest.

<< It is well to remark that insofar as he is in the cave, and even if he has already walked a long way towards the exit, to within a single step of the exit, *he has no idea of God.*

This is the part of the will in salvation. An effort in the void; an effort of the afflicted and blind will, for it is without light. >>

Once he has gotten out, he suffers again from the glare, but he is safe. (At least, indeed, as long as he does not act foolishly and go back into the cave, in which case, he would have to begin again.) There are no more efforts for the will to make, it is only necessary to keep oneself in a state of waiting and of looking at the light, as hard as that may be. When one waits and looks, time itself will give a greater and greater capacity of receiving the light.

There are two periods of confusion when one no longer knows where one is, when one believes oneself lost. The first one is in the cave, when, unbound, one has turned around and begun to walk. The second one, much more agonizing, is when one leaves the cave and is shocked by the light.

These two periods correspond exactly to the two "dark nights" that St. John of the Cross discerns, the dark night of the senses, and the dark night of the spirit.

[It is quite difficult to think that this comparison that is so precise, is not anything but the condensation of generations of mystical experience.]

The final moment, when the delivered one looks at the sun itself, the good itself, that is to say God himself as he is, corresponds to what St. John of the Cross calls the spiritual marriage.

But in Plato this is not the end. There is still one more step. (This is also indicated by St. John of the Cross.)

Republic VII, 519c–520e

>   Our business as founders of the city is to force the better natures to
>   arrive at the supreme knowledge, that is to say, at the vision of the
>   good, and to ascend that mount; but once they have ascended, we
>   cannot allow them the license that they now have, namely, that of
>   remaining on high without wishing to descend again to the captives
>   and taking part in the more or less contemptible labors and honors
>   that go on there. The law is not interested in the exceptional success
>   of one category of citizens, but in establishing, by persuasion and
>   by constraint, a harmony of all citizens based on the capacity of
>   each to serve the common good. The law produces such people in
>   the city not so that each one of them can turn and go where he wills,
>   but in order to make use of them *as a bond that unites the city*. We
>   are committing no injustice to those who have become philosophers
>   in our town, we will tell them with just words . . . We have begotten
>   you to the end that you might be for yourselves and your co-
>   citizens the chiefs and queen bees. We have raised you better and
>   more perfectly than the others, we have made you fit for both kinds
>   of life. You need therefore to go back down, each of you in turn,
>   into the home common to all, and get used to seeing in the shadows.
>   For once you are used to it, you will see a thousand times better
>   than those down below; you will understand each of the appear-
>   ances, you will know what each appearance is of, and that is because
>   you have seen the truth about the just, true, and good things. And
>   thus, you and we, together, will live in this city *in a state of wake-
>   fulness, and not that of a dream, seeing what is actually the case*; for
>   the majority of cities (i.e., souls) are inhabited by people who en-
>   gage in shadow fighting and partisan struggle in order to take power
>   as if this were a great good. Here is the truth: the city where those
>   who ought to command are the ones who least want to command
>   is the best city, and the most peaceful, ++ [non-active action] ++ and
>   it is just the opposite for the city where the commanders are of the
>   opposing disposition. When we say this to those we have raised,
>   will they disobey? It is impossible, for we are imposing just obliga-
>   tions on just people.

It is necessary to remember that this city is a fiction, a pure symbol
that represents the soul. ++ Plato himself says so: "It is in heaven per-

haps that there is a model of this city for whoever wants to see it, and seeing it, to found a city of his own self." ++

The different categories of citizens represent the different parts of the soul. The philosophers, the ones who leave the cave, they are the supernatural part of the soul. << The whole entire soul needs to be detached from this world, but it is only the supernatural part that comes into relation with the other world. >>

When the supernatural part has seen God face to face, it is necessary that it turn itself towards the soul to rule over it, so that the whole soul may be in a state of wakefulness, whereas for all those in whom deliverance has not been accomplished it is in a state of dreaming.

<< The natural part of the soul, detached from one world, while attaining another that is beyond it, is *in the void* during the operation of deliverance. It is necessary to put it in contact with this world that belongs to it, but the right kind of contact, one that is not an attachment >>

To sum up, after having torn the soul from the body, having traversed death to go to God, the saint needs in some way to incarnate himself in his own body so that he might shed upon this world, upon this earthly life the reflection of the supernatural light. So that he might make of this earthly life and this world a reality, for until then it is only dreams. It is incumbent upon him thus to achieve creation. << The perfect imitator of God first of all disincarnates himself, then incarnates himself. >>

At this point, we need to ask how the one who has just left the cavern contemplates in order that his soul might get accustomed to the light? Clearly there are several ways. Plato indicates one of them in the *Republic*. This is the intellectual way.

In order to pass from the shadows to contemplation of the sun, intermediaries, μεταξύ, are needed. The different ways are distinguished by the intermediary chosen. In the way described by the *Republic*, the intermediary is relation.

The role of the intermediary is in the first place to be situated midway between ignorance and the fullness of wisdom, between temporal becoming and the fullness of being.

<< (between, in the manner of a mean proportional, for it is a question of the *assimilation* of the soul to God) >> Then, it is necessary that it *draw the soul towards being*, that it *call for thought*. In the intellectual

way, what calls for thought is having to face contradiction. Said otherwise, it is a matter of relation. For everywhere where there is the appearance of contradiction there is a correlation of contraries, which is relation. Every time that a contradiction is imposed on the intelligence, it is forced to think of a relation that will transform the contradiction into a correlation, and by that process the soul is drawn higher. For example: *Theaetetus.* The knuckle bones (4, 6, and 12).

Thus mathematics is the science of these kinds of relations. There are four branches: arithmetic, geometry, astronomy, and music (the last two are mathematical science, but ones of observation. Cf. The question of Plato on the stars.).

> It is the deliverance from the chains, the conversion from the shadows to the artificial objects (puppets), and the light and the ascent outside the cave to the sun and there, in the moment of impotence of looking at animals, plants, and the light of the sun, it is the looking at divine images and real things reflected in the water. There are no more shadows or puppets . . .
> The sciences that we have just mentioned are effective in this way for leading what is most precious in the soul to contemplate what is most excellent in being. (VII.532b–c)

What comes after these sciences? It is something that Plato calls "dialectic," but he is quite reticent here. It consists in seeking to *give an account* of the sciences themselves. It is necessary

> without the help of any sensation, by pure reason, to strive towards what each thing is in itself, and not to stop before having seized by the intelligence itself what the good itself is. (VII.532a–b)

Further on, he says:

> The sciences, which we have said, participate in being—geometry and those like it—we see that they see in some way the subject of being, as in a dream, but are incapable of seeing it unveiled. This is because they use hypotheses (i.e., axioms and postulates) that are

not examined, and cannot be when giving an account. The dialectical method alone dispenses with hypotheses and directs the eye to the principle itself. (VII.533b–d)

After that, one is reduced to intuiting from a few scattered pointers.
Greece had a *mysticism or mystical contemplation that bore on mathematical relations. Very singular.* Cf. Proclus on Plato and Philolaos.
<< *Contemplation of the world a priori.* >>
It seems clear that the way that goes from the mathematical sciences to God seen as the good has to pass through the notion of the order of the world (not though as a thing as given by empirical observation), of *the beauty of the world.* The few indications that we can get elsewhere are pretty much related to this notion.
<< Contemplation of the order of the world a priori >>
These indications are:

1st. A text of Anaximander
The birth of things comes from indeterminate matter, and destruction works as a return to indeterminate matter, by virtue of necessity; for things undergo a mutual punishment and expiation towards each other, because of their injustices, according to the order of time. [DK 12 B 1]
2nd. An unfathomable text: A mysterious passage from the *Gorgias* of Plato:
. . . It is necessary not to let the desires be insolent or to try to fill them; there is an inextinguishable evil, one that leads to the life of a thief. One taking this way cannot be a friend of God or man; for one cannot thus form any commonality (κοινωνία), and where there is no commonality there is no friendship. The sages affirm, Callicles, that what holds heaven and the earth together, and gods and men, is community and friendship and order (κοσμιότητα) and restraint and justice; and for this reason they have called this whole an "order," my friend, not disorder, or intemperance. It seems to me that you do not pay attention to this whole, whatever else you might know. *You do not see that geometric equality has a great power with both gods and humans.* You think that it is necessary

always to work on acquiring more above all. What you forget is geometry. (507e–508a)

(Cf. "Justice is a number equally equal.") [DK 58B 4 22–23.]

3rd. A still more mysterious passage from the *Philebus* (16b–e)

++ [Give examples from music and letters] ++

There cannot be a more beautiful way than this one. I have always loved it, but often it escapes me and leaves me abandoned and not knowing what to do. It is not hard to explain, but it is very difficult to practice. *All the inventions that are connected to an art or a technique have always come from it.*

It is a gift from the gods to human beings, it seems to me; and a Prometheus has made it come down from the dwelling of the gods at the same time as a very brilliant fire. And the ancients, better people that we, and living closer to the gods, have handed on this tradition; namely, that things that we call eternal proceed from the one and the many and are innately both limited and unlimited.

<< [NB it is not a question here of the world, but of an *eternal order* from which the world proceeds.] >>

Since these things are thus ordered, we ought in each of our researches to start with a single idea. We will find it, for it is implied in the search. If we find it, after this unity it is necessary to examine two [branches], if they are [in the matter studied], unless there are three or more; and then divide in the same way the unity of each of these branches; then we will see on this originally unitary subject not only that it has unity and an indefinite many, but also what number it has. The idea of the unlimited ought not to be applied to quantity, until we have seen clearly in this matter the exact number that is the intermediary between the one and the unlimited. Only then is it necessary to allow the unity in each matter to be lost in the unlimited. The gods have given us this method for searching, to instruct us, and for teaching . . .

(We no longer know how to apply this.)

Examples. Grammar—Voice—a multitude of sounds emitted by the voice—Knowing how many letters and which ones.

Music.

Similarly, the inverse way, going from the unlimited to the one. Thoth, the inventor of letters, first of all began with the vowels and then the consonants and then the mutes; counted all of them; and gave them the common name of letters.

Further on: (26b)

"It is from these two types of things that the seasons and all that is beautiful have been produced from us, namely, from the mixture of unlimited things and those which involve a limit."

<< Note that here appears the notion of *beauty*—Read here the passage from the *Symposium* >>

It is necessary to remark:

1st. This theory is specifically Pythagorean (cf. Philolaos and Pherekydes), but the Pythagoreans, whose origins hardly go back a century, cannot be these "ancients" of whom Plato speaks. It is therefore a matter of an even more ancient tradition, such as Orphism or the Eleusinian mysteries.

This tradition comprises both a theory of primitive inventions (writing, music, certain techniques), a theory of invention in general, and a theory of the order of the world. The whole thing rests on a single principle, namely, the mixture of the unlimited and the limited. This principle equally constitutes a moral principle (in the same dialogue) [and, in the *Statesman*, a principle of politics].

2nd. Plato, apropos of this tradition, alludes to Prometheus. Aeschylus presents Prometheus as the author of the first inventions, of the knowledge of the seasons, of the revolutions of the stars, and of number.

Without forcing these correspondences, one can remark:

—That this notion of the order of the world is very closely related to the wisdom books (but more precise).

—That the words ἀριθμός, number, and λόγος, relation, are used indifferently for each other in the Pythagorean tradition. Λόγος can mean "word," but it can also mean "relation." The One in Plato is God, the unlimited is matter. Hence the saying "NUMBER CONSTITUTES THE MEDIATION BETWEEN THE ONE AND THE UNLIMITED" has singular resonances.

In the same way: "the seasons and all that is beautiful have been made by the mixture of the unlimited and the limited"—which is to say, by the ordering principle.

<< (All that is beautiful, i.e., all things insofar as they are beautiful. For the universe is beautiful—cf. the *Timaeus*.) λόγος is for the Greeks essentially the mixture of the limited and the unlimited. EUDOXUS. >>

Finally, do not forget that Prometheus, who is at stake here, is a god who has taken lightning from Zeus in order to give it to human beings, out of love for human beings, and this caused him to be crucified. See what lightning is in the *Hymn* of Cleanthes. St. Luke 12:49: "I came to cast (βαλεῖν) fire on earth, and how it is that I wish that it had already taken place?" (Cf. also the analogy between: "double-edged" and "I did not come to bring peace but a sword.") This passage shows that the fire of Prometheus was not material fire. That begins with a theory of the fall and of original sin and an image of life in God. *Acts of the Apostles*: tongues of fire.—St. Matthew, word of St. John the Baptist: "He will baptize you with the Holy Spirit and fire—"

The dialogue where the notion of the order of the world appears most clearly, and where it is found personified in a divinity who is named the "soul of the world," is the *Timaeus*.

But before going on to the *Timaeus*, it is necessary to linger, on the notion of beauty and love, the other way of salvation that Plato indicates, the non-intellectual way, the way of love. *Phaedrus, Symposium*.

(This is saving love—Plato describes in the *Republic* its opposite, the love that destroys, infernal love, what he calls "tyrannical love.")

The *Phaedrus* indicates a way of salvation that is not intellectual in the slightest degree, that has nothing to do with study, with science, with philosophy, it is salvation by feeling alone, and at the beginning an entirely human feeling; the love that consists in falling in love.

This is the doctrine of Platonic love that has had such prodigious fortunes and that has impregnated so many countries. *Europe*, Arabs.

The entire soul is immortal [proof: it is the principle of movement].

With respect to its structure, this is what needs to be said about it: To describe it wholly would be an enterprise both divine and long; but to express it like this would be human and less onerous: [246a]

[There follows a comparison showing very great antiquity. For one finds it in Hindu texts that are probably contemporaneous with Plato.

This image therefore ought to show there was a time when the people of the two countries were a single people.]

It is necessary to compare the properties that belong to a winged chariot and to a driver. With the gods, both the horses and the driver are all good and come from good stock; with everybody else there is a mixture. And, above all, the driver in us drives a pair of horses; and of these horses one is beautiful and good, born of good and beautiful parents; the other one is its opposite. Thus, by necessity, driving our team is difficult. Here is the origin of immortal and mortal beings. All that is soul has care for what is without soul, and courses through the heavens although in ever changing forms. The perfect and winged soul moves through the sky and governs the whole world. The one that has lost its wings is carried down until it meets something solid that it can inhabit; it takes an earthly body. (246a–c)

[In Greek, nature generally means *essence*]
[It is impossible to say more clearly that the wing is *a supernatural organ, which is to say, GRACE.*]

It moves in the upper regions, where the race of the gods dwells, and, of bodily things, it is that which is the most like the divine. The divine is beautiful, wise, good, and all that follows from that. These virtues are particularly the ones that nourish and enhance the winged part of the soul: ugliness, evil, and all that is contrary to these virtues exhaust it and make it perish. Zeus, the great sovereign of the sky, advances in the front, leading his winged chariot, ordering and surveying all things. He is followed by the army of gods and of daemons ranged in eleven ranks. Hestia remains alone in the house of the gods . . . Whoever wants to do so, can follow. Various are the displays of happiness and the movements inside heaven where the blessed race of the gods go, each doing his own work. Whoever wants to do so can follow. There is no envy in the divine choir. *When they go to eat, to feast,* they ascend and go to the highest vault of heaven. The chariots of the gods, well-balanced, and with good reins, rise easily, the others with difficulty. For the vicious horse is heavy; he tends toward the earth by virtue of his weight whenever the driver has not trained him well. That imposes a great difficulty on the soul, and an extreme violence (ἀγὼν). The souls of those that we call immortals, having arrived at the summit, go out and stand on the outer rim of heaven and allow themselves to be carried around by its rotation, while they look upon all that is beyond the heavens.

The world that is beyond the heavens, no poet has ever sung nor will one sing of it worthily. Here is how it is. For it is necessary to dare to speak the truth, always, but above all when one is speaking of the truth. The really real is without color, without form and without anything that one could touch; it cannot be contemplated except by the master of the soul, by the mind (νοῦς). It is this that is the object of true knowledge, which also dwells in this place. (ἀληθοῦς ἐπιστήμης γένος). 246d–247d

++ [NB Here again, Zeus, Being, Knowledge. Zeus feeds on being, and this act of eating constitutes knowledge. Zeus feeds on being, which is to say, God is fed by God. "Nourishment" here means both love and joy.] ++

In the same way that the thought of God is fed by mind and knowledge (νοῦς καὶ ἐπιστήμης) without admixture, so also the thought of every soul that is on the point of receiving what is fit for it, when it learns reality, across time, it loves (ἀγαπᾷ) and it contemplates and it is fed by the truth and it is happy until the rotating movement has brought it back to the same point.

++ God feeds on God. ++

In the course of this circular voyage it sees justice itself, reason, knowledge; not what we call knowledge, not the knowledge that is produced and that changes with circumstances, but the knowledge that is really in essence its reality [ἀλλ' ἐν τῷ ὅ ἐστιν ὂν ὄντος]. And in the same way, it contemplates and feeds on the other real realities; then, sliding back to the inside of heaven, it returns home. (247d–e)

++ The soul FEEDS ON God. ++

<< [NB one sees clearly here what the Platonic ideas are. They are purely and simply *the attributes of God*.] >>

Such is the life of the gods. Among the other souls, the better ones follow God, are like God, and lift the head of the driver into the world that is beyond the heavens; and they are borne along in the circular movement of the heavenly sphere. But the soul is troubled by the horses, and it has difficulty in contemplating being. It rises and it falls because of the violence of the horses, and it sees certain things and not others.

The other souls all aspire to follow on high, but they cannot, for they are submerged and carried along and trample on each other in trying to get ahead. Thus there is a lot of tumult, mixing it up, and sweat. So, because of the incompetence (κακίᾳ) of the drivers, many of the horses are lamed, and many wings are broken. All of them suffer great difficulty and go away without having attained ++ (ἀτελεῖς, uninitiated, without having been initiated) ++ the contemplation of reality. *And when they depart, they go to the fodder of opinion.* This is why there is such zeal to see the field of truth, where truth resides; one finds there the nourishment that is fit for the better part of the soul that comes from this meadow, and this nourishment is the essence (φύσις) of the wing that makes the soul light. And this is an ironclad law (νόμος Ἀδράστειας, i.e., Nemesis). The soul following God who learns something of the truth (τι τῶν ἀληθῶν) is beyond harm until the next revolution. If it can always do this, it is always secure. But when, being incapable of following, it does not see, when by virtue of some accident (τινι συντυχίᾳ χρησαμένη) it has been burdened with forgetfulness and evil, that burden causes it to lose its wings and fall to earth.

[Then it submits to human generation—It dresses itself with such or such a personality—(philosopher, king, businessman, artisan, tyrant, etc.; the theory of castes with additions) according to what it has seen on high, before its fall, more or less of truth.] [*there are no slaves* in this list]

The soul that has never seen the truth never dresses in human form. For it is necessary that one should be able to comprehend by reasoning in conformity to an idea that reasoning cuts through a

multitude of sensations (δεῖ γὰρ ἄνθρωπον ξυνιέναι κατ᾽ εἶδος λεγο-
μένον, ἐκ πολλῶν ἰὸν αἰσθήσεων εἰς ἕν λογισμῷ ξυναιρούμενον).
For this constitutes the memory of the things that our soul has seen
when it was following God, when it saw (ὑπεριδοῦσα, transcendent
vision—saw supernaturally—*saw above and beyond itself*) that reality on which we stand, and emerged (ἀνακύψα) into the really real.
(249b–c)

[Thus every human being, without any exception, and this includes the most degraded of slaves, has a soul that comes from the world
above the heavens, which is to say, from God, and that is called to return
there. The sign of this origin and this calling is the ability to form general ideas, without which no infant could learn to speak. Among human
beings there are only accidental and variable differences in degree here.
Essentially, they are identical, and hence equal. The Pythagoreans defined justice by equality. This idea of the essential equality of all people
insofar as they are children of God, goes back at least 2,000 years before
the Christian era, for one finds it in Egyptian documents that are this
early.]
    This theory of reminiscence is Orphic, which is proved by "the cold
water that gushes from the lake of Memory."
    What is meant by these words "reminiscence" and "memory"? It is
clear as soon as one brings his attention to bear on the image itself,
which is always necessary to do in these comparisons. If I have a thought
. . . then two hours later forget it . . . and then turn my attention to the
void; towards the void, but towards the real, then the thing is suddenly
there, no question about it. I did not know it, and now I recognize it as
being what I was waiting for. It is a fact of daily life, and an unfathomable mystery.
    We naturally only have concepts of the realities of this world. The
past is real at our level, but it is not within our reach, and we cannot take
even one step towards it. We can only orient ourselves for some emana-
tion that comes to us from it.
    This is why the past is the best image of eternal realities, of super-
natural realities. [Joy, the beauty of remembering is perhaps connected
to this. Proust had seen into this.]

<< This comparison can help us to seize the relation between sensible things, particulars and the eternal. For the past, it exists in objects that we call memories—a letter, a ring, etc., because they constitute for the soul a contact with the past, a real contact. The sacraments . . . >>

Here is now the usefulness of the *madness of love* (Plato's expression) for salvation. It is a question of a love that is first generated as carnal love. But above all it is a question of the grace that comes from the effects of beauty, and one can transpose this for every type of sensible beauty.

As we were saying, every human soul by the fact of its essence (φύσει) has contemplated reality, otherwise it would never have entered into a human being. But it is not easy for every soul to remember things up there, either because it saw them only for a short time, or because once it fell down here it was beset by affliction; for example, the affliction of being turned towards injustice by certain associations, which makes it forget the holy things that it had seen elsewhere. (249e–250a)

[Forgetting; another image of unfathomable depth: What we have forgotten of our past—e.g., an emotion—absolutely does not exist. And yet the things of our past that we have forgotten keep their full reality, the reality that belongs to them and that is not existence, for today the past does not exist, but is a past reality.]

There are few souls who retain much memory. These, when they see here an image of things beyond, are thunderstruck (ἐκπλήττονται) and lose self-control. They do not know what is happening to them, because they do not distinguish it adequately. With respect to justice, to wisdom, and to other values (τίμια ψυχαῖς), their images here below do not shine with anything emanating from them; only a small number of people, by means of dull instruments and with difficulty, go towards these images and contemplate the essence (γένος) of that which is represented. But beauty was resplendent (λαμπρόν) to see back then, when with the choir of the blessed we contemplated this happy spectacle and were initiated into those mysteries that are appropriately called the most blessed of mysteries, those mysteries that we celebrated when we were pure, not having yet suffered any evil. Someday we will return there, and we will be initiated into those whole and simple and unchanging and blessed visions (φαίνω), and we will contemplate, we will officiate (ἐποπτεύοντες) in a pure splendor, being ourselves pure and no longer being marked by what we now carry around with us, what we call the body, this thing to which we are attached like an oyster to its shell. The joys that are produced by memory! But let us keep on, pushed, thanks to memory, by the regret of things that were seen before. With respect to beauty, as we have said, it is resplendent, accompanying other beings; and when we come here below, we seize upon her by the senses. WISDOM IS NOT VISIBLE. FOR OTHERWISE IF THERE WERE GIVEN A CLEAR IMAGE OF THE WISDOM THAT PENETRATES THE EYES IT WOULD PRODUCE TERRIBLE LOVES. But the fact is that beauty alone has this destiny (mission?) of being at one and the same time that which is most evident and most desirable (ἐρασμιώτατον). The one who has not been recently initiated or who has been corrupted is not immediately transported from this world into the other one towards beauty itself whenever he contemplates here whatever bears its name. He does not venerate it when he sees it, but abandons himself to a beast-like lust and tries to go away from it. But the one who has recently been initiated, who has regularly contemplated the things above, when he sees a godlike face or some other corporeal form, one that portrays beauty well, above all he shudders and something of the terrors (δειμάτων) of the other world [the terrors of the fall] come back to him, and then gazing on it he venerates it as a god . . . And while he gazes there is produced in him, like the shivering of a fever, an upheaval, a sweat, an unfamiliar heat. This is from receiving the outflow of beauty by the eyes. This outflow warms him and waters the wings' essence (φύσιν). The warming dissolves what was found around its root, and which, being closed for so long by its hardening (σκληρότητος), prevented its growth. Under this surge of nourishment the shaft enlarges and takes on an impulse to push out from the root into all that constitutes the soul (ὑπὸ πᾶν τὸ τῆς ψυχῆς εἶδος). For formerly the whole soul was winged.

++ Cf. *the winged love* of the Orphics. ++

During this period the whole soul is seething and [ἀνακηκίει, to gush, to ooze—πέτρης, from a rock, trickle, breathe out, spread—ἀνά on high] gushing. And the same suffering happens to it as to infants who are teething. When the teeth begin to emerge, their gums tingle and are irritated. This is the sort of suffering that the soul undergoes when the wings begin to grow. It boils, it is irritated, it tingles, it itches, all the while that they are growing. (250a–251c)

The shock of beauty is what the Republic *calls that which makes the chains fall off and which forces one to walk.*

All this is not simply an image, it is really a theoretical essay in psycho-physiology on the phenomena that accompany grace. There is no reason not to attempt such a theory. Grace comes from on high, but it falls upon a being who has both a psychological and physiological nature, and there is no reason not to give an account of what is produced in these natures by contact with grace.

Plato's idea is that beauty has a double action, first as a shock that provokes the memory of another world, and then as the material source of an energy directly usable for spiritual progress. [Warmth, nourishment: these images indicate energy] The objects are sources of energy, but energy at different levels. For example, in war a medal is really a source of energy, in a physical sense, literally, at the level of military courage.

<< Money, for *work*. >>

In a general way, every object of desire is a source of energy, and the energy is at the same level as the desire. Beauty in itself is the source of an energy that is at the level of the spiritual life, and that is because of the fact that the contemplation of beauty implies detachment. Something that is seen as beautiful is something one ought not to touch, something that one does not want to touch for fear of harming it. In order to transmute usable spiritual energy from the energy from other objects of desire, an act of detachment is needed, an act of refusal—refusing the medal, giving money. However, the attraction of beauty implies in itself a refusal; it is an attraction that keeps its distance. Thus the beautiful is a machine to transmute base energy into elevated energy.

This analysis is transposable to every type of spiritual progress. Wherever there is love there is sensible beauty. A religion is inconceivable without symbols and these symbols are beautiful. The Eucharist acts on the soul by a beauty that is analogous to works of art. Virtue or the sanctity of a human being appears on the outside as a sensible beauty in the expression of the face, or in gestures, or attitudes, or the voice, or in some manner of one's bearing. Sciences enclose a sensible beauty. Etc.

There is no real love where the part of the soul that is most closely attached to the body does not play a role, and the good can only come to it in the form of the beautiful.

Irritation, tingling of the gums. Admirable image. Here again, the irreducible role of suffering. The simile is admirable because this sprouting and the pain of sprouting are produced without one's being able to explain what is going on and without any direct role in producing it. The will can only do one thing: look at the beautiful and not throw itself upon it. The rest is accomplished despite the will. From this point of view, this image is better even than that of the cave.

> This itching in the wings, in the absence of the beloved, is a violent pain:
> The channels through which the wings push up are dried up and closed and hinder the growth of the wing. What is inside them, full of desire but closed in, beats like a pulse in an inflamed sore; it pierces these channels like a needle. Thus the whole soul everywhere is stung (κεντουμένη) as if bitten by a gadfly and tortured. *At the same time, having the memory of beauty, it is full of joy.*
> [When it sees the beautiful, the part where the wings are pushing is soothed], it has a respite from the prickings and the tortures, and tastes for a time the sweetest of delights. (251d–e)

This also can be transposed. Cf. St. John of the Cross on the alternation of the periods of the dark night and of sensible grace.

The soul recovers a memory of the god that it followed above and whose image it sees in the beloved. This memory is at first quite imperfect.

> He seeks and tries to find in himself the image of his god. *He succeeds because he is forced to gaze continually towards his god.* He enters into contact with him by memory. The god enters into him and he takes into himself the god's habits (ἔθη) and teachings that make it possible for a human to participate in divinity. (252e–253a)

The lover tries to make the beloved as much like this god whose memory he has found again as possible, and when the beloved responds to this love, there is established between the two of them a friendship founded on a common participation in divine things.

But the itching of the wings is not the only suffering that one has to undergo in the course of this process. There is another suffering that is more violent.

[This is because of the evil horse, who wants to throw himself on what is beautiful. The unruly horse, not caring about either bridle or whip, drags the lover towards the beloved by violence. But once in the presence of the beloved, the memory of the essence of beauty returns to him.]

"Seeing beauty, the soul fears, it reveres (σέβομαι) and it falls back, and reins in the horses so violently that the horses sit back on their haunches, the one with no resistance, the other despite himself. Then both retreat . . ." (254b–c).

But once again the bad horse drags the chariot towards the beloved. The same experience comes upon the driver as before, and more intensely. It is as if he were recoiling before a barrier. He violently jerks back on the bit in the mouth of the wanton horse, bloodying his jaws and tongue, knocking him back on his legs and flanks onto the ground, and laying torments on him. When the vicious horse has undergone this treatment time and again, he is humiliated and obeys the will of the charioteer; and then, when he sees the beauty before him, he nearly dies of fear. (254d–e)

Here, as in the image of the cave, is an irreducible quantity of suffering. And as in the cave, there are two distinct sorts of suffering; the one is voluntary, for it is the movement imposed on a body that is stiff, the blow of the whip laid on the bad horse; the other is entirely involuntary, and it is linked to grace itself, which, although it may well be the unique source of joy, causes suffering whenever the state of perfection is not attained. It is in the dazzling of the eyes, and the irritation of the wings.

Voluntary suffering has only a negative import, it is simply a condition—in order to define its nature, Plato uses an admirable image, that of training. This image is implied in the metaphor of the chariot, and this metaphor shows a staggeringly ancient origin, for it is also in ancient Sanskrit texts.

Training is based on what today is called conditional reflexes. By associating such or such a thing with pleasure or suffering, one develops new reflexes that end up being produced automatically. We can thus get the animal within us to behave in such a way so as not to trouble our attention when it is turned towards the source of grace. One trains circus dogs with whips and with sugar, but often it is quicker and easier with the whip; besides, one does not always have sugar. Suffering is therefore the chief means. But it has no value in itself. One can beat a dog all the day long without it learning anything. Sufferings that one inflicts are useful for nothing, and are even detrimental if they do not follow a method that is a function of the goal one is pursuing, namely, that the flesh does not get in the way of grace. The method alone is what is important here. It is unnecessary to give the animal within one more blow than the strict minimum to reach the goal. But not one less, either.

Note here that the bad horse is as much a help as a hindrance. He is the one who irresistibly drags the chariot towards the beautiful. When he is tamed, the itching in the wings is a sufficient motive for the charioteer. But at the beginning, the bad horse is indispensable.

His faults are useful, for each of his faults is the occasion of some progress in the operation of training. The simple accumulation of punishments leads him in the final account to a complete docility. It is well to note that training is a finite operation. The horse may well have a very difficult temperament, and can remain for a very long time without having made any progress, but we are absolutely sure that by punishing him time and again he will finally reach a perfect docility.

Such is the source of the security and the foundation of the virtue of hope. The evil that is within us is finite, as we are. The good by whose help we fight it is outside us and is infinite. Therefore it is absolutely sure that the evil will be vanquished.

Note that if this training is a voluntary operation, and thus a natural one, it is, however, only accomplished insofar as the soul is touched by the memory of things above and as the wings have begun to sprout. *And this is a negative operation.*

With respect to the grace that accompanies joy and sorrow, and is that which works salvation in us, this is something that we receive without having any part in it, excepting the necessity that we keep ourselves exposed to grace; this is to say, that we maintain our attention oriented towards the good with love. The rest, smooth or rough, works in us without us.

++ It is this second element that proves that this is a truly mystical operation ++

Once the bad horse is tamed, the lover, and by a contagious effect, the beloved, too, remember more and more of what is above. Here philosophy intervenes anew, but Plato does not say what sort of study he is thinking of.

He says a bit more in the *Symposium*, where a way is indicated, one by which, by love, we go towards the highest knowledge. Socrates, repeating the teaching of a woman of the greatest wisdom named Diotima, recommends, when one is seized by love for the beauty of a shape, a physical appearance, that we understand above all that beauty is not something that belongs to that appearance alone, but that it is also found in other physical appearances. Beauty is therefore something in which these appearances participate, but which itself does not appear, an invisible thing. From there one can rise to the consideration of beauty in actions (the virtues), then to that of the beauty in the sciences and in philosophical doctrines.

until one is plunged into a sea of beauty
oriented towards the immense sea of beauty. *Symposium* 210d
Here is the final point of this progression:

The one who has considered beautiful things in order and as is fitting, coming upon love's fruition, suddenly contemplates a certain beauty of supernatural (θαυμαστόν) essence; this is why one has taken all this trouble. It is eternally real, it neither comes to be nor does it perish, it neither increases nor decreases. It is not beautiful in one part and ugly in another, nor beautiful at one moment and not at another, nor is it beautiful from one angle and not from another, nor is it beautiful here and ugly there, nor is it beautiful for some and not for others. And where the beautiful itself is found it does not fade away, as is the case with faces, hands, and all corporeal

things, and all particular words, and each particular science. And it does not dwell in anything else, whether a living being, or heaven, or earth, or whatever other thing there might be. It is itself, it is a unique essence, it is eternally real. Other beautiful things participate in it, but in such a way that when they are born and when they perish, it does not receive, nor grow, nor diminish, nor undergo any other modification . . . When one comes face to face with this beauty, one has nearly arrived at the goal. When someone follows the order [of study] already indicated [that goes from the knowledge of individual beauties and leads to the knowledge of universal beauty] . . . then [one comes from] the knowledge of beautiful things to this knowledge, which is nothing other than the knowledge of the beautiful itself; thus one ends by knowing what the beautiful is . . . Let us dream about what it is to see the beautiful itself, intact, pure, not filled and soiled with human flesh and colors and all this mortal foolishness, but the beautiful itself, in its unique essence, if one could see it! . . . [He who can . . .] having touched the truth, engendering and nourishing in him true virtue, will become a friend of God and immortal inasmuch as can be given to a human being. (210e–212a)
In this matter, human nature can hardly find a better help than Love (ἔρως). This is why I say that all people ought to honor Love. (212b)

This absolute beauty, divine, the contemplation of which makes one a friend of God, is God's beauty, it is God in his attribute of beauty. This still is not the end of it; that corresponds to being in the *Republic* (the Word).

It is not a question of a general idea of beauty. It is a question of something else. Something that is the object of love, of desire. Something that is eternally real. One gets there by discovering bit by bit what makes beauty, which is not carnal attraction, but harmony, and in searching with love for this harmony in all things.

This passage in the *Symposium* tells us what follows after geometry and astronomy in the way indicated by the *Republic*; this is the consideration of beauty in those sciences; and from this beauty one passes to the Good.

The search for *perfection* is the way of the *Symposium*.

Plato placed the way indicated by the *Republic* under Prometheus's patronage. He does not name any divinity in particular with respect to the way indicated in the *Phaedrus*; but he constantly uses, and with a very evident insistence, a set of terms that specifically belong to the terminology of the mysteries, both in the *Phaedrus* and in the *Symposium*. That and the term μανία used in the *Phaedrus* evoke the God of the mystical madness, the god of the mysteries, Dionysios—who is the same as Osiris, the suffering God, dead and come to life, judge and savior of souls. Prometheus and Dionysios are the soul's two guides to God.

In the *Symposium*, Love plays this role. Plato gives the theory of mediation in relation to him.

> Every demi-god (bad translation) is an intermediary (μεταξύ, proportional mean), between what is mortal and what is immortal—And what is his virtue (δύναμιν)? To interpret (ἑρμηνεῦον; Hermes is also a mediator!) and to communicate human things to the gods and divine things to humans, prayers and sacrifices on the part of humans, orders and responses to sacrifices on the part of the gods. He fills the space between humanity and divinity, so that everything is found to be connected through him. This is why the art of divination happens because of him, and the art of the priesthood, and sacrifices, and the mysteries, and incantations. God does not mingle with humans, but by this intermediary there is intercourse and dialogue between divinity and human beings. (202e–203a)

> The story of the birth of Love. Son of Abundance, that is, divine plenitude, and of Misery, that is, human misery. Poros (way, path, expedient, resource) was sleeping, drunk on nectar. Misery coupled with him while he slept . . . (surely this is a very old tradition, for the name of Poros in inexplicable—But in any case, this is God).

> (Love) is always miserable, dried out, thin, in rags, barefooted, without shelter, lying on the ground, without a bed, sleeping in front of doors and on the streets, in the open air, because due to his mother's nature he always has deprivation as his companion. (203c–d)

[Cf. The verses of Dante on poverty] The marriage of St. Francis with Poverty, the widow of Christ:

> While young, the lady for whom he began a war
> against his father is one to whom, like death,
> no one ever freely opens his door.
> And before her spiritual court
> in the presence of the Father, he became one with her
> and loved her more and more each passing day.
> She, missing her first husband,
> for eleven hundred years and more was hated and ignored
> and until him she had no suitors.
> It did not matter that she was fearless
> even before Pluto, even at the sound of his voice,
> the voice that induced fear in the whole universe.
> It did not matter that she was faithful and proud,
> that while Mary remained on the ground,
> she, with Christ, was lifted up on the Cross. (*Paradiso* Canto
> XI.58–70)

> Because of his father, though, he was enterprising with respect to everything that is good and beautiful, being audacious, active, always tensed, a formidable hunter . . . His nature is neither mortal nor immortal . . . *He dies, and he comes to life again through the nature that he shares with his father . . . He loves wisdom; for he was born of a wise and clever father, and of an ignorant and miserable mother . . .* (203d–204b)

The idea of mediation plays an essential role for Plato; for as he says in the *Philebus*, "*it is necessary to take care not to make the one too quickly.*"

Poros, the Superabundant, son of Wisdom . . . After the feast, Misery came to beg, as she always did on feast days, and she put herself near the doors. Poros, drunk with nectar, entering in the garden of Zeus, heavy and drowsy, fell asleep. Misery conceived of a plan, because of her destitution (ἀπορία) to have a child by Poros. She stretched herself out by him and conceived Love. (203b–c)

II. *The Creation. Timaeus*

This contains a second proof of God. The first corresponds to what Descartes called the proof from the idea of perfection. The second is the proof from the order of the world. This is not the proof that we ordinarily are given, that is, the adaptation of means to ends that is miserable and ridiculous. The only legitimate proof from the order of the world is the proof from the beauty of the world. The beauty of a Greek statue inspires a love that cannot have stone for its object. In the same way the world's beauty inspires a love that cannot have matter as its object. It comes down to the same thing: the proof of God by love. There cannot be any other ones, for God is not something other than the Good, and there is no other organ that can enter into contact with him except love. Just as one cannot recognize sounds by sight, in the same way, love is the only faculty that can recognize God.

This pure good has two reflections, one is in our soul and is the idea of the good, the other is in the world in its beauty. The order of the world *is* the beauty and not a definable order, just like when in a poem a word has been put in it for effect, the poem is mediocre . . . (Or the critic is mediocre who explains the poem this way . . .)

The *Timaeus* is a story of creation. It is not like any other dialogue of Plato, and it seems to come from somewhere else. Or Plato is inspired by a source unknown to us; or something has happened to him between the other dialogues and this one. What is easy to divine. He has left the cave, he has seen the sun, and he has returned to the cave. The *Timaeus* is the book of a man who has reentered the cave. Thus the sensible world no longer appears like a cave.

There is a trinity in the *Timaeus*; The Maker, the Model of creation, and the Soul of the World.

It is above all necessary in my eyes to make this distinction: What is eternally real being, without generation, and what is perpetual becoming, which never has reality? The one is grasped by thought with the help of reason (λόγος), a selfsame eternal reality, the other is believed by opinion and with the help of unthinking sensation what is becoming and perishing, without ever really being. Moreover, that which is made (γιγνόμενον) necessarily has an author (αἰτίου τινός), for it is quite impossible that there be something made without a maker. Thus, whenever the Maker, who always looks towards that which is conformed to itself, using it as his model, reproduces its essence (ἰδέαν) and virtue (δύναμιν), necessarily something of perfect beauty is made. If he looks towards becoming, using as his model what comes to be, the result is not beautiful. (27d–28b)

<< Very obscure lines when one does not have their key, but luminous when one does. The key is that Plato is giving a theory of artistic creation, or by analogy, of divine creation. >>

In order to interpret these lines well, it is necessary to understand that Plato has in mind, as an analogous image of divine creation, the image of artistic creation; the composition of a poem, the sculpting of a statue, etc. These lines contain the complete theory of artistic composition, an experimental theory. If an artist tries to imitate either a sensible thing, or a psychological phenomenon, a sentiment, etc., the work will be mediocre. In the creation of a work of art of the first order, the attention of the artist is oriented towards silence and the void; from this silence and this void descends an inspiration that is worked out in words and forms. The Model here is the source of transcendent inspiration — and it follows that the Maker corresponds well to the Father, the Soul of the World to the Son, and the Model to the Spirit.

<< The Model is ultra-transcendent, and non-representable, like the Spirit. >>

No particular intention. The poet who uses a word for effect is a mediocre poet.

This Model is a Living Being, not a thing.

++ It is a well-chosen analogy if the proof of the divine origin of the world is its beauty. Why is this image more legitimate than that of a clock? It is that a work of art — like understanding and like love — contains *inspiration*. These lines frame the distinction *between art of the first order*, which necessarily has a relation to sanctity, and art of the 2nd, 3rd, and nth order. Many of those who are looked upon as very great artists belong to the art of the 2nd order. ++

Now, whether it is the whole heavens, or this world or whatever name we give to it, it is necessary in the first place to ask of it, as one ought to with respect to no matter what subject is at hand, if it is an eternal reality, having no principle of generation, or if it has come to be, beginning from some principle. It has come to be for one can see it, touch it, it has a body, and everything that belongs to sensations and sensible things, that opinion grabs onto aided by sensation, has come to be and is manifestly the subject of becoming. The creator (ποιητής) and father of this universe is a great thing to discover; when we have found him, we cannot speak of him at all.

But it is still necessary to inquire of this subject on which of the two models the Worker built the world, whether it was after the model that remained conformed and identical to itself or whether it was based on the model that changes (γεγονός). If the world is beautiful, if the craftsman is good, it is clear that he looked towards the eternal. In the other case, which it is not even permitted to mention, he looked towards that which changes. It is quite manifest that he looked to the eternal. For on the one hand, this is the most beautiful of created things, and on the other, he is the most perfect of authors. Being born this way, it is clear that he has built on a model that thought and relation can grasp, one that is something that is self-identical. (28b–29a)

Let us now say why there was becoming and why the author composed what he did. He was good, and in him who is good there is never any envy. Being without envy, he wanted all that was begotten to be as like him as possible. God wanted that everything might be good (φλαῦρον δὲ μηδέν εἶναι κατὰ δύναμιν), that no thing should be deprived of its proper value. Thus he took all that there was of the visible (πᾶν ὅσον ἦν ὁρατὸν παραλαβών), which was then all in chaos, always moving without rhythm and without order. He then brought it from disorder to order, judging that order is absolutely [πάντως] better than disorder [i.e., better in itself, not with respect to any relation]. The most perfect being has not had and does not have the license to do anything other than the most beautiful thing. On reflection he understood that among the things of visible essence a universe without intelligence could not be more beautiful than a universe where there is intelligence. It is impossible that intelligence might exist in any way without a soul. After this reckoning, it is by the union of an intelligence with a soul and of a soul with a body that he put together the universe, to the end of having accomplished something that in its essence was a perfectly beautiful work. Thus according to verisimilitude it is necessary to say that this world was in truth born with a soul and with intelligence by the providence of God. (29d–30c)

The Model:

In the likeness of which one of the two living beings did the maker compose things? Let us not deign to say that it was in the likeness of one of the beings that is a part of things. *For that which resembles the imperfect cannot be beautiful.* The living being of which all the others, considered separately or by species, are parts, is the being among all the others that we posit that the world is most like. This one embraces and possesses in himself all the living spiritual beings, as the world contains us and all visible animals. God wanted to make a unique living visible being that resembled this being, the most beautiful of spiritual beings (νοουμένων), perfect in all respects, having in its interior all living beings of the same species, and he made it. (30c–31a)

[A Unique World]

. . . to the end that in its unity it would be like the absolute living being, the creator did not create two universes nor an infinite number, but this heaven here, unique, the unique son (μονογενής), which was, which is, and which will be. (31b)

<< (Heaven, soul of the world). >>

[This heaven, i.e., intelligence united to the soul of the world (he says it later on) and not to the body of the world. This is what is *the unique son.* An expression that will recur.]

[Body, visible and tangible, whence comes fire and earth. Three dimensions, there it is necessary that there be two proportional means: air and water.]

In this way and by these four types of elements the body of the world is born, having been put in concord by the proportional mean; and for that reason it possesses friendship, of the sort that it holds together with itself and that makes it indissoluble. [32b–c] Such was the thinking of the eternally real God about the God who would be one day (the Word insofar as it is the orderer of the world). (34e)

The Soul of the World:

He put the soul in the middle, stretching it across the whole from the outside and wrapped the body (the soul is *outside* the body) and he made of it a circle turning around, a single heaven, alone and empty (οὐρανόν ἕνα μόνον ἔρημον) capable by its own power of being a companion to itself, having need of no other, known and loved sufficiently by itself. Then he begot it, a blessed God. (34c)

Composition of the soul of the world:

[The soul is not the νοῦς. It is the God engendered in its relation with the creation, at the intersection of the other world and this one as MEDIATOR.]

From indivisible substance, eternally identical to itself, and from that which is related to body, which is becoming and divisible, starting with these two substances, he made a third kind of substance as an intermediary, namely, the substance relative to the essence of the same and the other. And insofar as it is an intermediary he linked it by the same relation to the indivisible on the one hand and to the corporeal and divisible on the other. And taking these three realities, he combined all three of them into one unique essence [ἰδέαν], by forcing a harmony between the nature (φύσιν) of the Other, which revolts against blending, and that of the Same. (35a)

The base, the essence of the soul of the world is something that constitutes a proportional mean between God and the material universe. The proportional mean is the same idea as mediation.

This mediating function oddly enough brings together the Soul of the World of Prometheus, of Dionysios, of Love, and of the perfectly just man in the *Republic.* (Love in the Orphic texts plays the role of the Soul of the World.)

Orphic text on love (Aristophanes' *The Birds*) [vv. 693–702]
> There was in the beginning Chaos and Night and dark shadows and vast Tartaros.
> The Earth did not exist, nor the Air nor the Sky. In the unlimited bread of the shadows
> Night of the black wings bore an egg without seed (egg of the world, cf. *Phaedrus*).

> From that, when the seasons had gone round, grew Love desired,
> On his back, shone golden wings, like the whirlwinds,
> He, uniting with winged Chaos and night across (κατά) vast Tartaros,
> Made spring forth our race and was what caused it to rise to the light (ἀνήαγεν).
> There was no race of immortals, before Love had put all together.
> When things were combined with each other, then was born the Sky and the Ocean,
> and the Earth, and the imperishable race of the blessed gods.
>   (Cf. φιλία in the *Gorgias*—Love is the principle of order.)

Proclus, commentary on the *Timaeus* (32c) [=DK 7 B 3]
> Pherekydes (Pythagoras's teacher, a Syrian) said that Zeus changed himself into love when he was on the verge of creating, for he brought together the order of the world from contraries into a concordance (ὁμολογία) and brought it to friendship and planted in all things identity and unity, as is well known.

Another conjunction is that of suffering. There is suffering in Prometheus, Dionysios, Love (the impoverished Love, without a roof over his head), the Just Man. Notice here that of the Soul of the World:

(*Timaeus* 36b–37a)

> God cut this mixture [of the Same and the Other] lengthwise into two, crossing the halves over each other in the form of an "X" and curved them in order to join them into a circle, bringing together the extremities at a point opposite their intersection. He brought them into a uniform movement and on the same axis, a circular movement that enveloped them. He made one of the two circles to be the exterior and the other the interior. He decided that exterior rotation would be that of the essence of the Same, and the interior that of the essence of the Other, and he gave sovereignty to the rotation of the Same and of the Like . . . He stretched all corporeal being across the interior of the soul . . . it was thus that the visible body of heaven was given birth, and the soul, invisible and participating in relation and harmony, was born from the most perfect of eternally real thoughts, the most perfect of created thoughts.

(*Timaeus* 92c)

> . . . This world, a living visible being containing all that is visible, a sensible image of the spiritual God, is born, infinitely large, good, beautiful, and perfect, this only heaven, which is the only son.

CHAPTER FIVE

Notes on the Concept of Character

(Notes sur le caractère)

How one is a constant self is a classical philosophical and psychological problem. Weil shows an interest in it in varying degrees throughout her writings. These notes, likely written in the fall of 1941, are a concentrated look at the issue. Though brief and sketchy, they do continue interests shown elsewhere in Weil's philosophical writings of the period, such as how we can change our characters and our readings of the world, and how external circumstances can very much determine our selves, especially when we are under duress, even to the point of annihilating them. The text presented here is the result of combining two of the three variants of these notes.

Character: an invariant that supposes an identity throughout varied manifestations. There are categories of the concept we can never define, and the only reason we do not eliminate them is that we cannot get beyond them, either. To our mind, such an invariant is common not only in manifestations that are affirmed to take place in fact, but in ones that are simply possible, that might have taken place or that in certain cases could take place in the future. We ought to define what these possibilities are. But we do not have the faculty of enumerating these manifestations, of saying what is possible or what is impossible with respect to somebody of such and such a character. On the other hand, character is something constant over a period of time; the way a person is at a single moment does not at all reflect the character of this person; character is what is invariant through successive manifestations. We, however, do concede that character changes.

Style affords a comparison. There is a limit to possible ones. But in fact it is also nearly impossible to say that such or such a phrase might or might not be from a given author (Shakespearean criticism). There is a constant style through phrases written successively, and through successive works; however, the author has different ways of writing. One can neither define the concept of style nor do away with it.

There is a mystery in musical themes. A theme is an invariant. It cannot be defined, it cannot be done away with.

Character is an invariant that appears throughout the reactions of a human being (acts, gestures, attitudes, words), and, if it were itself defined, would define the possible reactions. It is always intuited from the *outside* (Kant). But not by the same givens. In the same way my voice for me and for others is different (phonograph). Which is the true voice? The question does not make any sense. The set of manifestations that we try to put together by means of an unvarying factor differs according to the people who are thinking about the character of such and such a person. If ten readers of a prolific author all read different works of his, they would all have a different opinion about his style. This was a theme exploited by Pirandello. Yet, one could not even think about a human being if one did not think that he really had a character that is the same through all his reactions, even though this character cannot be known by anybody. Like a cube . . . But with respect to character, there is no mathematical concept to help us out here. This is an impenetrable mystery, and yet we cannot pose a moral problem without putting the concept of character at its center. For although the reactions that in fact make a person something other than pure reason are undefined, unlimited, we cannot think about them without conceiving something definite in relation to them, something defined in principle but not defined in fact.

Given that character is an invariant common to the possible reactions of a single person and that limits his possible reactions, then, if we could define it, we would find: 1st a system of obstacles (Mehl) that hinder or make possible actions or thoughts in such and such a direction; 2nd a way of organizing one's attention that makes a human being impenetrable by certain things and very penetrable by others, which means that a given order of things exists or does not exist for such a being; 3rd a way of organizing time, a way of being a certain sort of person in relation to time.

The interesting problem from the moral point of view concerning character is the problem of how a character comes about. How is character modified by circumstances? How is it either conserved, despite circumstances, or modified in a determinate sense, with respect to its aspiration to the good? And (this is a problem identical to the previous one, but interesting with respect to short periods of time) how is a person led to act out of character with respect to evil or good in exceptional circumstances? What is the empire of circumstances, what is the power of liberty that can make someone act out of character or that might give him a different character?

I propose three hypotheses (for being that character is hypothetical, like the celestial sphere is, everything that concerns it is hypothetical also).

1st The reaction of a human being with respect to determinate circumstances that force him to get involved in some manner or other depends upon the circumstances and his character; the possibility of a choice is illusory. When we have to choose, the choice is in fact already made.

2nd External circumstances, including our own past actions, over which we have no control, continually exercise on character a modifying action more or less strong, sometimes momentary (when one "acts out of character"), sometimes enduring (when character changes.)

3rd Our own power (i.e., the power of what is free within us) of modifying our character is indirect; exactly in the same way as our power over matter, defined by work, is indirect. "What man becomes greater just because he wants to be?" It is exercised on the one hand by the possibility of putting ourselves in such and such circumstances that in the course of things will act on us from the outside (but then it is necessary at least to see ahead in some measure how they will act; there is a greater or lesser chance of inevitable error here). On the other hand, it is exercised by the orientation that we give to our attention in the moments that appear to be the most insignificant, the most indifferent moments of our lives, the moments that do not engage us, where circumstances do not solicit any choice from us.

1st. Courage, for example. We are often more or less courageous than we want to be. We *cannot* perform such an act of courage (and, in effect, there is a necessary complicity of the body)—[moral courage, not physical! bombardments]. We cannot keep ourselves from putting ourselves into danger . . .

How does one come to have the sort of courage that conforms to the judgment of our reason?

In the same way, generosity. Sometimes this . . . sometimes that . . .

(To speak truly, at the moment one would have liked to have done something other than one did.)

2nd—a difficult theme, because pride gets in the way. We hold onto our character, and do not want to believe that it could change. [Renunciation is the renunciation of character, for what one holds onto are the elements of character.] Difficult observation about oneself—about others.[1]

Our character appears to us as a limit by which we do not want to be imprisoned. We like to dream that someday we will be able to escape ourselves in one or more directions. We are happy to know that we can model our character, achieve it, go beyond it. But our character also appears to us as a support that we want to believe is unshakable. We want to believe that we are capable of never doing, saying, thinking certain things. Sometimes we are wrong. St. Peter.

Thus our problem with respect to our character is double. First of all, how can we modify it ourselves, model it, and go beyond it in the direction of the highest value? Then how can we keep the empire of circumstances in certain cases from breaking it and transforming it in such a way that we are exiled from ourselves? This second problem is difficult and agonizing. It is necessary to make an effort to pose it. What guarantee do we have that someday we will not become, despite ourselves, something that we hate, or at least something that is utterly foreign to us?

Elements of character—holding a greater or lesser place—that belong to *conditions*. E.g., factory workers—the condemned—foreign refugees [e.g., people looking for visas]—a slightly different example, but nonetheless . . . : communists. (Communism defines a *character*.)— Phenomena of uniformity.

In antiquity, above all in Rome, a phenomenon of this order, intriguing, but one that has not been studied. Perhaps the phenomena of this type elude us by their very nature . . . That is to say, slavery. A mass of slaves—dozens, hundreds, thousands—were free men who by accident fell into slavery. Before, they were very different sorts of people. Afterwards, there were very few differences between them. There is almost never a question about character when dealing with slaves. Plautus gives a quite exacting psychological analysis of slaves, but there appear to be few differences. There is never a question of their past. There appears in Plautus one characteristic of a slave; e.g., an obsession with punishments.

There is very rarely a question of too little docility on the part of slaves, according to the ancients, except in one sort of case that turns up frequently, but always with the same consequences. When circumstances came about wherein a certain number of slaves were liberated, masters could not get [unliberated] slaves to obey them (the revolt in Sicily follows from an occurrence of this sort). Thus as long as liberty does not feel like a possibility, slaves cannot disobey. Whenever they sensed that it was possible, they could no longer obey.

In Plautus, in all the stories of slaves, even subtle stories, there is an indifference to good and evil. (Not Epictetus, of course—however, there is the philosophy of a slave.) "Jupiter takes away half the soul of a man at the moment that he becomes a slave."

Las Casas—"The Spaniards took away the nature of Indian character to the point of making them inferior to the most timid of animals."

NOTE

1. This draft continues on with the following notes. By themselves, they are sketchy to the point of opacity. In their place, I have continued the text by adding a section from Weil's second draft of these notes that fills out a number of these allusions. (Ed.)

Corneille: rests entirely on the fiction of character devoid of circumstances (*Don Sanche d'Aragon! Pertharite*). Revenge of Corneille. But that is how all revenge is. Lies, *theatre*, ROLE.

Humility, perhaps the refusal of the lie, of this comedy (flaying, poverty . . .)
St. Peter
Death, *Asdrubal*. Ivan Ilych.

If one of us were to be executed in five minutes . . .
Affliction. Tacitus: life of Agricola.

Oedipus
— Lear — William II (cup of tea)
— Famine in Ireland
— Slavery in the ancient world
    Plautus. Peter P
Power. Roman emperors (Caligula. Titus. Domitian)
Gyges. 9th book of the *Republic* —
Spain (License)

CHAPTER SIX

What Is Sacred in Every Human Being?

(La Personne et le sacré)

This essay comes from Weil's last writings in London in 1943, while working for the Free French. It clearly continues and advances in very important ways her concerns about the human being that are evident earlier in the writings from Marseille. It is clear that she is targeting "Personalism," but it is not clear which Personalist she has in mind. For, along with her own very original alternatives, she clearly is critiquing somebody in particular. There is no question now about it being Jacques Maritain and specifically his book *The Rights of Man and Natural Law*, which was published in New York in 1942.[1] It is important therefore to realize that when she here criticizes the use of the term *personne*, "person" and its alternative translation, "personality," she has Maritain's use of it specifically in mind. She is not nearly so restrictive in using it herself elsewhere in her writings. Maritain's emphasis on the *personne* was far from anything like egoism. His understanding of it depended on a certain metaphysical self, though; it was the something in each of us that allowed "the expansiveness of being ... [which] in the depths of our ontological structure is a source of dynamic unity and of inner unification." Weil's mordant comments about the "expansion of the personality" deal with this idea of Maritain's. But in the end, Weil's philosophical concern is with the metaphysics and the limitations that basing treatment of others on the notion of the *personne* involves; the obligations, she thinks, that we owe others need no such grounding and have no such limitations.

"You do not interest me." These are words that one human being cannot address to another without cruelty or offending against justice.

"Your personality does not interest me." These are words that can have a place in an affectionate conversation between close friends without wounding what is most delicately sensitive in that friendship.

In the same way, one can say without abasement, "My personality does not count here," but never, "I do not count."

This proves that there is something wrong in the vocabulary of the stream of modern thought called "personalist." And in this domain, whenever there is a grave error in vocabulary, it is hard to avoid grave errors in thought.

There is in each human being something sacred. But it is not his person, which is not anything more than his personality. It is him, this man, wholly and simply.

There is a passerby in the street who has long arms, blue eyes, a mind where thoughts are swirling that I know nothing about, but that may well be nothing special.

It is neither his person nor his personality that is sacred to me. It is him. Him as a whole. Arms, eyes, thoughts, everything. I would not violate any of this without infinite scruples.

If the human personality were what is sacred for me, I could easily put out his eyes. Once he was blind, he would still have a personality. I would not have touched his person at all. I just would have destroyed his eyes.

It is impossible to define respect for human personality. It is not just impossible to define verbally. Many luminous ideas are like this. But this notion cannot even be conceived; it cannot be defined and outlined by the silent operation of thought.

To take as a rule of public morals a notion that is impossible to define and to conceive is to open ourselves up to all kinds of tyranny.

The notion of rights, launched across the world in 1789, was by its internal insufficiencies impotent to exercise the function that was given to it.

To join together two insufficient notions in speaking of the rights of the person will not get us any farther.

What is it that keeps me from poking out his eyes, if I am allowed to do so, and might even find it amusing?

Although he may well be sacred to me as a whole, he is not sacred in all respects and relations. He is not sacred to me insofar as his arms happen to be long, or insofar as his eyes happen to be blue, or insofar as his thoughts happen to be common. Nor, if he is a duke, insofar as he is a duke. Nor, if he were a garbage man, insofar as he is a garbage man. None of that would stay my hand.

What would stay it is knowing that if someone were to poke out his eyes that it would be his soul that was lacerated by the thought that someone had done evil to him.

There is at the bottom of every human heart something that goes on expecting, from infancy to the grave, that good and not evil will be done to us, despite the experience of crimes committed, suffered, and observed. This above all else is what is sacred in every human being.

The good is the only source of the sacred. There is nothing sacred except the good and what is relative to the good.

This profound and childlike part of the heart that always expects good is not what is in play when we claim our rights. The little boy who jealously watches to see if his brother has a piece of cake slightly bigger than his gives in to a motive that comes from a much more superficial part of the soul. The word "justice" has two very different meanings that are related to these two parts of the soul. The first is the one that matters.

Every time that the childlike cry of Christ himself, "Why have you hurt me?," cuts into the bottom of the human heart, there is certainly injustice. And if, as often happens, that hurt was only the result of a mistake, injustice then consists in the lack of an explanation.

Those who inflict blows that provoke this cry give in to different motives according to their characters and according to context. Some people find this cry at certain moments to be sensuous. Many are unaware that things went so far. For this is a silent cry that sounds only in the secret place of the heart.

These two states of mind are closer than they seem. The second is but a weaker version of the first. This ignorance is complacently maintained because it flatters and contains in it a sort of sensuousness also. There are no limits to our wills other than the necessities of matter and the existence of other human beings around us. All imaginary expansion of these limits is self-indulgent, and thus there is a sensuousness in all that makes us forget the reality of these obstacles. This is why upheavals, such as war and civil war, that empty human existences of their reality, that seem to make puppets of them, are really intoxicating. This is also why slavery is so pleasant to the masters.

For those who have undergone too many blows, such as slaves, this part of the heart that inflicted evil makes them cry out in surprise, seems dead. But it never is entirely. It just cannot cry anymore. It is ensconced in a state of dumb and uninterrupted moaning.

But even for those whose ability to cry out remains intact, this cry almost never expresses itself inside or out in words that can be followed. Most often, the words that try to translate it fall completely short.

That is even more inevitable as those who most often have the sense that evil has been done to them are those who know least well how to speak. Nothing is more frightful, for example, that seeing in a courtroom some unfortunate stammering before a judge who is making clever jokes in elegant language.

Excepting the intelligence, the only human faculty truly interested in the liberty of public expression is this part of the heart that cries out against evil. But as it does not know how to express itself, liberty is a small thing for it. It is above all necessary that public education be such that it furnishes, as much as possible, the means of expression. Then it is necessary to have a regime where the public expression of opinions is defined less by freedom and more by an atmosphere of silence and attention wherein this weak and inept cry can make itself heard. Finally, a system of institutions that brings out, as far as possible, leaders who can and want to hear and understand this cry.

It is clear that a party occupied with trying to get or trying to keep governmental power cannot discern anything but noise in these cries. It will react differently according to whether this noise hinders its own propaganda or whether, on the contrary, it enlarges it. But in any case, it is not capable of a tender and divining attention that can discern the significance of this cry.

The same thing is the case to a lesser degree for the organizations that imitate, by contamination, the parties, which is to say, when public life is dominated by the competition of the parties; all organizations are included here, including, for example, the unions and even the churches.

To be sure, parties and similar organizations are also strangers to intellectual scruples.

When the freedom of expression is reduced in fact to the freedom of propaganda for organizations of this type, the only parts of the human soul that deserve expression are not free. Or, their freedom is infinitesimal, hardly more than in a totalitarian system.

Now, this is the case in a democracy where the competition of the parties determines the distribution of power, which is how it is with us, the French, and it is what we call democracy. For we do not know anything else. It is necessary to invent something else.

The same criterion, applied in an analogous manner to all public institutions, can lead to some equally obvious conclusions.

The "person" does not provide this criterion. The cry of sorrowful surprise that rises up from the bottom of the soul upon the infliction of evil is not something personal. A blow to the person and his desires is not enough to make it burst forth. It always bursts forth by the sensation of some contact with injustice through pain. It is always, just as it is in the case of Christ, in the case of the least of men, an impersonal protest.

It is also raised very often in cries of personal protest, but those do not matter; one can provoke as many of those as one wants without ever violating the sacred.

What is sacred in a human being is that which is, far from the personal, the impersonal.

Everything that is impersonal in a human being is sacred, and that alone.

In our time, where writers and scientists have so strangely usurped the place of priests, the public recognizes, with a complacency that is not founded on reason, that the artistic and scientific faculties are sacred. This is generally considered as obvious, however far this may be from actually being the case. When one believes that one needs a motive, one alleges that the playing out of these faculties is among the most exalted forms of expanding the human personality.

Often, in effect, that is all that it is. In this case, it is easy to make an accounting of what this is worth and what it yields.

This yields attitudes towards life such as those, which are so common in our century, expressed by the horrible phrase of Blake: "It is better to suffocate a child in his crib than to keep within oneself an unsatisfied desire."[2] Or such as that which has given rise to the conception of the gratuitous act. This gives us a science where all the possible norms, criteria, and values are recognized, except truth.

Gregorian chant, Romanesque churches, the *Iliad*, the invention of geometry were not, in the beings through whom these things passed in order to come down to us, occasions of the expansion of personality.

The science, art, literature, and philosophy that are only forms of personal expansion constitute a domain where dazzling and glorious successes are accomplished and make names that will live for thousands of years. But above this domain, far above it, separated from it by an abyss, is another domain where things of the first order are situated. These are essentially anonymous.

It is only by accident that the names of those who have penetrated there are saved or lost; even if the names are saved, they themselves have entered into anonymity. Their person has disappeared.

Truth and beauty inhabit this domain of impersonal and anonymous things. This level holds what is sacred. What is at the other level does not, or if it does, the sacred appears only like a splash of color might, which in a painting represents the Eucharist.

What is sacred in science is truth. What is sacred in art is beauty. Truth and beauty are impersonal. All that is too obvious.

If a child does addition, and if she fails, the error bears the mark of her personality. If she proceeds in a perfectly correct manner, her person is absent from the whole operation.

Perfection is impersonal. The person in us is the part in us of error and sin. Every effort of the mystics has always sought to reach the place when there is no longer anything in their soul that says "I."

But the part of the soul that says "us" is still infinitely more dangerous.

Passage into the impersonal only comes about by attention of rare quality, and is only possible in solitude. Not only actual solitude, but moral solitude. It is never accomplished by those who think themselves members of a collectivity, as part of an "us."

Humans in a collectivity do not have access to the impersonal, even its lesser forms. A group of human beings cannot even do addition. Addition works in a mind that has forgotten for a moment that other minds exist.

The personal is opposed to the impersonal, but there is a way from one to the other. There is no way from the collective to the impersonal. It is necessary above all that a collectivity be dissolved into separate persons in order that they may enter into the impersonal.

In this sense only, the "person" participates more fully in the sacred than the collectivity does.

Not only is the collectivity foreign to the sacred, but it misleads us by offering a false imitation of it.

The error that attributes a sacred character to the collectivity is idolatry; this is the crime that is most widespread in every time and every country. The one in whose eyes expansion of the personality alone counts has completely lost even the sense of the sacred. It is difficult to know which of the two errors is worse. Often they are combined in the same mind in varying doses. But the second error has less energy and staying power than the first.

From the spiritual point of view, the struggle between the Germany of 1940 and the France of 1940 was principally a struggle not between barbarism and civilization, not between good and evil, but between the first error and the second. The victory of the first is not surprising; it is by itself the stronger of the two.

The subordination of the person to the collectivity is not a scandal; it is a fact in the order of mechanical facts, like that of a gram to a kilogram on a balance. The person is in fact always under the weight of the collectivity, up to and including what is called the expansion of the personality.

For example, it is precisely the artists and writers who are the most inclined to regard their art as an expansion of their person, who are, in fact, the most in thrall to public taste. Hugo never had any difficulty in reconciling the cult of the self and the role of "sonorous echo." Examples such as Wilde, Gide, or the surrealists are still clearer. The scientists situated at the same level are also slaves of fashion, which exerts more power in science than it does on the shape of hats. The collective opinion of specialists is nearly sovereign on each and every one of them.

Being subject in fact and by the nature of things to the collective, the person has no natural rights relative to itself.

One is right to say that antiquity did not have the notion of respect due to the person. It thought far too clearly to have such a confused conception.

A human being only escapes the collective by being elevated above the personal in order to penetrate into the impersonal. At this moment there is something in him, a portion of his soul, on which nothing of the collective can have any grip. If he can root himself in the impersonal good, which is to say, if he becomes capable of drawing energy from it, he is in a state, every time that he thinks that he has an obligation to do so, of turning a small but real force against no matter what collectivity, without calling on any outside force.

There are occasions when a nearly infinitesimal force is decisive. A collectivity is much stronger than a single man; but every collectivity in order to exist needs operations that can only be accomplished by a single mind in a state of solitude, operations of which elementary arithmetic is a prime example.

This need opens up the possibility of the impersonal getting a grip on the collective, if only we knew how to learn a method to make use of it.

Each of those who have penetrated into the domain of the impersonal encounters there a responsibility towards all human beings. It is the responsibility of protecting in them, not their persons, but all the fragile possibilities that the personal has covered over of passing into the impersonal.

It is to this above all that the appeal for respect towards the sacred character of human beings needs to be addressed. In order that such an appeal might have an existence, it is quite necessary that it be addressed to whatever beings are capable of hearing it.

It is useless to explain to a collectivity that in each of the single beings that compose it there is something that it ought not to violate. Above all, a collectivity is not someone, except by a fiction; it has no existence, except abstractly; talking to it is a fictional operation. Moreover, if it were someone, it would be someone who is only disposed to respect himself.

Furthermore, the greater danger is not the tendency of the collective to curb the personal, but the tendency of the personal to throw itself into, to drown itself in the collective. Or perhaps the first danger is only the apparent and deceitful aspect of the second.

If it is useless to tell the collectivity that the personal is sacred, it is also useless to tell the personal that it is sacred. It cannot believe that. It does not sense itself to be sacred. The reason that keeps us from doing so is that it is in fact not.

If there are a few beings whose conscience testifies differently, to whom their person does give a certain sense of the sacred that they believe themselves to have, they are doubly deluded in generalizing and attributing it to every "person."

What they experience is not an authentic sense of the sacred, but a false imitation of it produced by the collective. If they experience it through their own person, this is because it participates in the collective prestige through the social consideration of which it finds itself to be the site.

Thus it is in error that they think that they can generalize. No matter that this generalization comes from a movement of generosity, it cannot have enough power to make their eyes stop seeing anonymous human matter as being anonymous human matter. But it is difficult for them to take this into account, for they do not have any contact with anonymous human matter.

In a human being, the personal is a thing in distress, it is cold, it runs about looking for a refuge and for warmth.

Those for whom it is warmly wrapped in social consideration or those who are waiting for this consideration do not know this, though.

This is why the philosophy of personalism has been given birth and spread, not in the populace in general, but in the milieux of writers who, by profession, possess or hope to acquire a name and a reputation.

The relations between the collectivity and the personal ought to be set out with the sole object of removing what is capable of preventing the growth and germination of the impersonal part of the soul.

For that to happen, it is necessary, on the one hand, that there be space around each person, a degree of free disposition of one's time, possibilities of going to higher and higher degrees of attention, of solitude, of silence. It is necessary at the same time that it be kept warm, in order that distress not constrain it to drown itself in the collective.

If that is the good, it seems difficult to go farther in the direction of evil than modern society has, even in democracies. Notably, a modern factory cannot be very far from the limits of horror. Each human being in them is continually harassed, prodded by the intervention of foreign wills, and at the same time the soul is cold, in distress, and abandoned. A man needs a warming silence, he is given an icy uproar.

Physical labor, though it may well be painful, is not in itself degrading. It is not art and it is not science; but it is something else which has a value that is absolutely equal to art and science. For it gives an equal possibility of gaining access to an impersonal form of attention.

To put out the eyes of an adolescent Watteau and to make him turn a millstone would not have been a greater crime than to take a youth who has a vocation for this kind of work and put him on the line in a factory or on a machine and pay him by piecework. It is only that this vocation, unlike that of a painter, is not discernible.

Exactly in the same measure as art and science, so physical labor, although in a different way, is a certain contact with reality, truth, the beauty of the universe, and with the eternal wisdom that constitutes the order of the universe.

This is why debasing labor is a sacrilege in exactly the same sense as trampling the Eucharist is sacrilege.

If those who labored were to sense it, if they were to sense that in fact they are the victims of sacrilege, that they are the accomplices of sacrilege, their resistance would have an entirely different spirit than what the notions of the person and of rights can give them. It would not be a claiming of anything; it would be an uprising of the whole being, fierce and desperate like a young girl that someone is trying to force into a brothel; and it would be at the same time a cry of hope coming from the bottom of the heart.

This feeling indeed dwells in them, but it is so inarticulate that it is indiscernible even to themselves. Professional wordsmiths are quite incapable of giving expression of it to them.

When someone speaks to them of their lot, generally one chooses to speak to them about salaries. They, under the fatigue of being weighed down and for whom every effort of attention is painful, welcome with relief the easy clarity of numbers.

They thus forget that the object that they are bargaining about—the one they complain that someone is forcing them to hand over cheaply, the one someone is refusing them a just price for—is nothing other than their soul.

Imagine that the devil is in the process of buying the soul of some poor afflicted being, and that someone, taking pity on the one afflicted, were to intervene in the debate and say to the devil: "It is really shameful for you to offer only this price; the thing is worth at least twice that."

This sinister farce is what is being played out in the workers' movement by the syndicates, parties, and intellectuals of the left.

This spirit of haggling was already implicit in the notion of rights that the men of 1789 imprudently put at the center of the appeal that they wanted to shout out in front of the world. This was to destroy in advance the power of that appeal.

The concept of rights is linked to that of sharing out, of exchange, of quantity. It has something of the commercial to it. It evokes legal proceedings and pleadings. Rights are always asserted in a tone of contention; and when this tone is adopted, force is not far behind to back it up, otherwise, it would be ridiculous.

There are a number of notions, all in the same category, that are in themselves entirely foreign to the supernatural and are, however, a bit above brute force. They are all relative to the mores of the beast of the collective, to use the language of Plato, as long as he keeps some traces of a discipline imposed upon him by the supernatural operation of grace. When they are not continually renewed by this operation, when they are only its survivors, they find themselves by necessity subject to the caprices of the beast.

The notions of rights, of the personal, of democracy, are all in this category. Bernanos had the courage to observe that democracy does not give any defense against dictators. The personal is by nature subdued by the collectivity. Rights are by nature dependent on force. Lies and errors that veil these truths are extremely dangerous because they keep us from having recourse to that which alone is found to be free of force and that can preserve us, namely, another kind of force, the shining of the spirit.

Weighty matter is only capable of overcoming gravity through the sun's energy that green leaves have captured in plants and that then operates in the sap. Gravity and death progressively but inexorably take back the plant that is deprived of the light.

Among these lies is that of natural rights, which was launched by the materialist eighteenth century. Not by Rousseau, who was a lucid and powerful spirit, and who came from a truly Christian inspiration, but by Diderot and the Encyclopedists.

The notion of rights comes to us from Rome, and, as with everything that comes from ancient Rome, who is the woman full of blasphemous names that the *Apocalypse* talks about, the one who is pagan and unbaptizable. The Romans, who understood, like Hitler, that force is not fully effective unless it is dressed in certain ideas, employed the concept of rights in this way. It lends itself to it very well. Modern Germany has been accused of scorning the idea of rights. But it made use of it to the fullest degree in its claims to be a proletarian nation. It did not recognize, it is true, that those it subjugated had any other right than that of obedience. The same was true of ancient Rome.

To praise ancient Rome for having bequeathed to us the concept of rights is singularly scandalous. For if one wants to examine what this notion in its cradle was for them, in order to discern its type, one needs to see that property was defined by the right of use and abuse. And in fact the greater part of the property to which the right of use and abuse applied was human beings.

The Greeks did not have the concept of rights. They did not have the words to express it. They were content with the name of justice.

It is by a singular confusion that one could assimilate the unwritten law of Antigone to natural rights. In Creon's eyes, there was absolutely nothing natural in what Antigone did. He judged her to be insane.

If anybody could consider him wrong, it is not us, we who, at this moment, think, speak, and act exactly as he did. We can verify this by looking at the text.

Antigone says to Creon: "It is not Zeus who published this mandate; it is not the companion of the gods in the other world, Justice, who had established similar laws among mortals." Creon tries to convince her that his orders were just; he accuses her of having disgraced one of her brothers while honoring the other, since the same honor had been accorded to the impious and to the faithful, to the one who died while trying to destroy his own country and to the one who died defending it.

She says: "Nevertheless the other world demands equal laws." He, showing good sense, objects, "But there is no equal division between the brave and the traitor." She only finds this answer absurd: "Who knows if this is a legitimate division in the other world?"

Creon's observation is perfectly reasonable: "But an enemy, even after he is dead, is never a friend." But the little naïf responds: "I was born to join, not in hate, but in love."

Creon, then, who is getting more and more reasonable, says: "Go, therefore to the other world, and then since it is necessary for you to love, love those who live below."

In effect, this was the right place for her. For the unwritten law that this little girl obeyed was far from having anything in common with any rights, or with the natural; it was nothing other than the extreme love, the absurd love, that pushed Christ onto the Cross.

Justice, the companion of the gods of the other world, prescribed this excess of love. No right prescribes it. Rights do not have any direct link with love.

As the notion of rights is foreign to the Greek spirit, it is also foreign to the Christian inspiration, at least where it is not mixed with the Roman heritage, or the Hebrew or the Aristotelian. One cannot imagine St. Francis talking about rights.

If one said to somebody who was capable of hearing, "What you are doing to me is not just," one could hit upon and uncover at its source the spirit of attention and love. It is not the same thing with words such as "I have the right to . . . ," "You have no right to . . ."; enclosed in these words is a latent war, and they reveal a spirit of war. The concept of rights, put at the center of social conflicts, makes any nuance of charity impossible there on both sides.

It is impossible, when one makes use of such a concept, to keep one's eyes fixed on the real problem. A peasant, whom a buyer in a market puts undue pressure on to get him to sell his eggs cheaply, can very well answer: "I have the right to keep my eggs if no one offers me a good enough price." But a young girl who is in the midst of being forced into a brothel will not speak of her rights. In such a situation, the words would seem ridiculously not up to the situation.

This is why the social drama, which is analogous to the latter situation, has appeared in a false light by using the word "rights" in a way analogous to the former situation.

The use of this word has turned what ought to be a cry spewing forth from the bottom of one's entrails into a bitter nagging for retribution, without purity or effect.

From the fact of its mediocrity, the concept of natural rights entails that of the personal, for rights are relative to personal things. They are situated at this level.

Adding the word "rights" to that of "person" implies the right of the person to what one has called its "expansion," and in that one has committed a very grave evil. The cry of the oppressed then descends even lower than the tone of a legal claim, it takes on the tone of envy.

For the person only is enlarged when social prestige inflates it; its expansion is a social privilege. One does not say this to the masses when speaking to them about personal rights, one tells them just the opposite. They do not have at their disposal a sufficient analytic power so that they could recognize that for themselves; but they sense it, and their daily experience makes them certain of it.

This is not for them a reason to reject this slogan. In our age of darkened intelligence, one does not have any difficulty in claiming for everybody an equal share in social privileges, in things that are essentially privileges. This is a type of legal claim that is at once absurd and low; absurd, because privilege by its very definition is something unequal; low, because it is not worthy of being desired.

But the category of men who formulate claims, and everything else, who have a monopoly on language, is a privileged category. They are not the ones who are going to say that privilege is not anything worth wanting. They do not think that. But anyhow, it would be indecent for them to say it.

Many indispensable truths that could save human beings are not spoken for this sort of reason; those who could speak them cannot formulate them, those who could formulate them cannot say them. The remedy for this evil should be one of the pressing problems of a true politics.

In an unstable society, the privileged have uneasy consciences. Some of them hide it behind an air of defiance and say to the masses: "It is entirely fitting that I have privileges and you don't." Others will tell them with an air of benevolence: "I claim for all of you an equal share in the privileges that I possess."

The first attitude is odious. The second lacks good sense. It is also far too easy.

Both of them urge the people to run down the path of evil, to be distanced from their one and true good, which is not in their hands, but which, in one sense, is so close to them. It, which is the source of beauty, truth, joy, and fullness of life, is closer to them than those who give them their pity. But not being there, and not knowing how to get there, everything happens as if they were infinitely far away. Those who speak for them, to them, are equally incapable of understanding what distress they find themselves in, and what fullness of good is at their door. And, for them, the people, it is indispensable that it be understood.

Affliction is by itself inarticulate. The afflicted silently beg that somebody give them words to express themselves. There are ages where those supplications are not granted. There are others where they are given words, but badly chosen ones, for the people choosing them are strangers to the affliction they are interpreting.

They are most often far from it by virtue of the place where circumstances have put them. But even if they are near to it, or if they have been inside it for a time in their lives, even recently, they are nevertheless strangers because they make themselves strangers to affliction as soon as they can.

Thought revolts from thinking affliction as much as living flesh revolts from death. A deer coming forward step by step freely and voluntarily to give itself to the teeth of a wolf pack is no more possible than an act of attention that is directed towards one who is really afflicted and nearby is by a mind who has the ability to avoid him.

What is indispensable for the good is impossible by nature, but it is always possible supernaturally.

Supernatural good is not a sort of supplement to natural good, as certain people would like, with Aristotle's help, to persuade us of to our great comfort. It would be nice if that were so, but it is not so. In all the pointed problems of human existence, there is only a choice between supernatural good and evil.

Putting words in the mouth of the afflicted that belong to the middle region of values, such as democracy, rights, or person, is to give them a present that is not open to leading them to any good, and that inevitably makes for much evil.

These notions do not have their place in heaven, but are suspended in midair, and for this reason they cannot get any sort of bite on the ground.

Only the light that falls continually from the sky gives a tree the energy to push powerful roots into the earth. The tree is actually rooted in the sky.

Only that which comes from heaven is capable of really making a mark on the earth.

If one wanted to arm the afflicted effectively, it is only necessary to put in their mouths words whose proper abode is in heaven, beyond the skies, in the other world. It is necessary to give them only words that express the good alone, a good and a pure state. Discrimination here is easy. The words that can be joined to something that also designates an evil are strangers to pure good. One expresses blame when one says: "He is putting his personality into play." The "person" is a stranger to the good. The possession of a right implies the possibility of using that right for either good or bad. Rights are therefore alien to the good. On the contrary, the accomplishment of an obligation is always good, everywhere. Truth, beauty, justice, compassion are always good, everywhere.

When it is a question of the aspirations of the afflicted, it suffices, in order to be sure that one is saying what is needed, that one keep to words and phrases that always express, everywhere, in every circumstance, good alone.

This is one of the two services that one can render them using words. The other is to find words that express the truth of their affliction; that, through all external circumstances, render sensible the cry always interjected into the silence: "Why has someone done evil to me?"

For that, they ought not to count on people of talent, on personalities, celebrities, nor even on people of genius in the sense that the word is ordinarily used, which confounds it with "talent." They can only count on the geniuses of the first order, the poet of the *Iliad*, Aeschylus, Sophocles, Shakespeare, such as he was when he wrote *Lear*, and Racine when he wrote *Phèdre*. That does not make up a very big number.

But there are a number of human beings, who, being poorly endowed by nature or mediocre, appear infinitely inferior not only to Homer, Aeschylus, Sophocles, Shakespeare, and Racine, but also to Vergil, Corneille, and Hugo, and who, nevertheless, live in the kingdom of impersonal goods where all of these latter writers have never penetrated.

A village idiot, in the literal sense, who really loves the truth, even when he only babbles, is in his thinking infinitely superior to Aristotle. He is infinitely nearer to Plato than Aristotle ever was. He has genius, whereas the word "talent" belongs to Aristotle. If a fairy came to him and proposed changing his lot for a destiny like Aristotle's, the wisest thing for him would be to turn it down without hesitation. But he does not know that. No one tells him it. The whole world tells him just the opposite. It is necessary to tell him. It is necessary to encourage the idiots, people without talent, people of mediocre talent or only slightly better than average, who have genius. There is no fear of making them proud. The love of truth is always accompanied by humility. Real genius is nothing else than the supernatural virtue of humility in the domain of thought.

In place of encouraging the flourishing of talent, as was proposed in 1789, it is necessary to cherish and rekindle with tender respect a belief in genius; for only the truly pure heroes, the saints and the geniuses, can be of help to the afflicted. Between the two, people of talent, intelligence, energy, character, strong personality, and the afflicted, is a screen that prevents help. It is not necessary to go after the screen, but it is necessary to put it carefully to the side, while trying to make sure that as little as possible is seen of it. And it is necessary to break the much more dangerous screen of the collective, while suppressing every part of our institutions and our mores where whatever form of party spirit dwells. Neither the personalities nor the parties ever give a hearing either to the truth or to affliction.

There is a natural alliance between truth and affliction because both are mute suppliants, eternally condemned to remain without voice before us.

Like a vagabond, accused in a court of having taken a carrot from a field, who stands before a judge who is comfortably seated and keeps up a patter of elegant questions, commentaries, and jokes, so much so that the vagabond cannot even get out a stammer, so the truth stands before a mind that is elegantly lining up its opinions.

Language, even in the case of one who appears to be saying nothing, is always that which formulates opinions. The natural faculty that we call intelligence is relative to opinions and to language. Language enunciates relations. But it expresses only a few of them, because it takes place in time. If it is confused, vague, hardly rigorous, disordered, if the mind that puts them forth or listens to them has only a weak ability to keep a thought in front of itself, it is devoid or nearly so of all real content about relations. If it is perfectly clear, precise, rigorous, orderly, if it addresses itself to a capable mind, having conceived a thought, of keeping it present to itself while it is thinking another thought, of keeping both of them present to itself while it thinks yet a third, and so on, in this case, language can be relatively rich in relations. But as with all rich things, this relative richness is a miserable atrocity compared to the perfection that alone is desirable.

Even when it puts things well, a mind enclosed in language is in prison. Its limit is the number of relations that words can render present to it at the same time. It remains in ignorance of thoughts implying a greater number of relations; these thoughts are beyond language, unformulatable, no matter how perfectly rigorous and clear they may be and no matter how the relations that went into them were expressible in perfectly clear terms. Thus the mind moves in a closed space of partial truth, which can be more or less big, without ever being able to cast a glance on what is beyond it.

If a captive mind ignores its own captivity, it lives in error. If it recognizes it, even if for a tenth of a second, and if it is pressed to forget it in order to avoid suffering, it lives a lie. Extremely brilliant people of intelligence can be born, live, and die in error and falsity. In these people the intelligence is not a good or even an advantage. The difference between people more or less intelligent is like the difference between prisoners condemned to life in prison whose cells are more or less large. An intelligent man who is proud of his intelligence is like a prisoner who is proud of having a big cell.

A mind that senses its captivity wants to deny it. But if it has a horror of lying, it will not do that. It is then necessary that one suffer a great deal. He will pound his head against the wall until he knocks himself out; he will come to, look at the wall with fear, and then one day he will start all over again and knock himself out one more time; and so on, without end, without any hope. One day he will come to on the other side of the wall.

Perhaps he will still be a captive, just in a larger place. What does it matter? He henceforth has the key, the secret that will make the walls fall down. He is outside what people call intelligence, he is where wisdom begins.

Every mind enclosed by language is only capable of opinions. Every mind that has become able to seize thoughts that cannot be expressed because of the multitude of relations that they combine, thoughts, however, that are more rigorous and luminous than what the most precise language expresses, every mind that has arrived at this point already dwells in the truth. Certitude and faith without shadow belong to it. And it hardly matters that it had its origin in a small or great intellect, whether it had been in a small cell or a large one. What alone matters is that having arrived at the limit of its own intelligence, whatever that might have been, it has gone beyond. A village idiot is nearer to the truth than a child prodigy. Both are separated from it only by a wall. We do not enter into the truth without having passed through our own nothingness; without having sojourned for a long time in a state of extreme and total humiliation.

It is the same obstacle that blocks us from understanding affliction. As the truth is something different than opinion, affliction is something other than suffering. Affliction is a mechanism for pulverizing the soul; the man who has been seized by it is like a worker who has been pulled into the cogs of a machine. He is nothing more than a torn and bloodied thing.

The degree and the nature of suffering that constitutes genuine affliction differ greatly among human beings. It depends above all on the quantity of vital energy one has when it starts and on the attitude one adopts before suffering.

Human thought cannot understand the reality of affliction. If someone were to recognize the reality of affliction, he would have to say: "The play of circumstances, over which I have no control, can snatch anything from me anytime, including everything that belongs to me and that I consider as being me. There is nothing to me that I cannot lose. An accident can at any time wipe out what I am and can indifferently put in its place any vile and contemptible thing."

Thinking that with the whole soul is to experience nothingness. It is the extreme and total state of humiliation that is also the condition for the passage into the truth. It is a death of the soul. This is why the sight of naked affliction causes in the soul the same jerking away that the nearness of death causes in the flesh.

We piously think of the dead when we evoke them only with the mind, or when we are walking among tombs, or when we see them suitably laid out on a bed. But the sight of dead bodies that are strewn over a battlefield, with a look to them that is both sinister and grotesque, is a cause for horror. Death appears in its nakedness, not dressed up, and the flesh shivers.

When distance or material or moral conditions let us see affliction only in a vague and confused way, without distinguishing it from simple suffering, affliction inspires a tender pity in generous souls. But when accidental circumstances suddenly reveal it in its nakedness as something that destroys, a mutilation or leprosy of the soul, we shiver and recoil. And the afflicted experience the same shivering of horror when faced with themselves.

Listening to someone is to put ourselves in his place while he is speaking. Putting ourselves in the place of a being whose soul is mutilated by affliction, or who is in imminent danger of becoming such a being, is to annihilate one's own soul. It is more difficult than suicide would be for a happy child. Thus the afflicted are not heard. They are in a state like that of someone who has had his tongue cut out and who momentarily has forgotten his infirmity. Their lips move but no sound comes to anyone's ears. They themselves rapidly become impotent in using language because of the certitude that they are not heard.

That is why there is no hope for the vagabond before the judge. If through his babblings something heartrending comes out that pierces the soul, it will not be heard by either the judge or the spectators. It is a mute cry. And the afflicted themselves are nearly always as deaf to each other. And each afflicted being, under the constraint of general indifference, tries either by lying or unconsciousness to make himself deaf to himself.

Only the supernatural operation of grace can make a soul pass through its own annihilation to the place where it gets the sort of attention that alone permits being attentive to the truth of affliction. It is the same attention in both cases. It is an intense, pure attention, without motive, and that is gracious and generous. This attention is love.

Because affliction and truth in order to be understood both need the same attention, the spirit of justice and the spirit of truth are one. The spirit of justice and of truth is nothing other than a sort of attention that is pure love.

By an eternal disposition of Providence, everything that one produces in every domain when he is controlled by the spirit of justice and truth is dressed in the radiance of beauty.

Beauty is the supreme mystery here below. It is a radiance that entices attention, but does not give it any motive for enduring. Beauty always promises and never gives; it creates hunger, but it has no nourishment for the part of the soul trying here below to fill itself; it only nourishes the part of the soul that gazes. It creates desire, and it gives the clear sense that there is nothing in it to desire, for one wants that nothing in it should change. But should one not look for ways to get out of the delicious torments that it inflicts, then this desire bit by bit is transformed into love, and it forms a seed of the faculty of pure and gracious love.

To the degree that affliction is hideous, so is the true expression of affliction supremely beautiful. One can give examples, even from recent centuries: *Phèdre*, *l'École des Femmes*, *Lear*, the poems of Villon, but even more so are the tragedies of Aeschylus and Sophocles; and even greater still are the *Iliad*, *Job*, and certain popular poems; greatest of all are the stories of the Passion in the Gospels. The radiance of beauty is shed on affliction by the light of the spirit of justice and love, which alone permits human thought to gaze upon and reproduce affliction as it is.

Every time that a fragment of inexpressible truth passes into words that, although they are not able to contain the truth that inspired them, have by their order a perfect correspondence with truth that furnishes support to every spirit that wants to find it. Every time this happens, the radiance of beauty is shed on those words.

Everything that proceeds from pure love is illumined by the radiance of beauty.

Beauty is sensible, although very confusedly and mixed with false imitations, in the interior of the cell where all human thought is first imprisoned. Hers is the only help that truth and justice with a cutout tongue can hope for. She has no language; she does not speak; she says nothing. But she does have a voice to cry out. She cries out and shows the justice and truth that are without voice. She is like a dog barking in order to get people to come to where his master is lying unconscious in the snow.

Justice, truth, and beauty are sisters and allies. With three words so beautiful there is no need to go looking for other words.

Justice consists in standing guard so that evil is not done to human beings. Evil is done to a human being when one cries from deep inside: "Why has someone done evil to me?" He is often deceived when he tries to say what the evil is, or who has hurt him, or why it has been inflicted on him. But the cry is never wrong.

The other cry that we often hear, "Why does he have more than I do?," is related to rights. It is necessary to distinguish the two cries and to take care of the second as much as one can, with the least brutality possible, using the help of the legal code, ordinary courts, and the police. In order to form minds capable of resolving problems within this domain, a law school suffices.

But the cry "Why has someone done evil to me?" poses entirely different problems, problems to which the spirit of truth, justice, and love are indispensable.

In every human soul the plea that evil should not be done to it rises up continually. The text of the Lord's Prayer addresses this plea to God. But God only has the power to preserve the eternal part of the soul that has entered into real and direct contact with him. The rest of the soul, and the whole soul of those who have not received the grace of real and direct contact with God, is abandoned to the will of men and to the accidents of circumstances.

Thus it is up to human beings to stand guard so that evil might not be done to human beings.

When evil is done to someone, evil really penetrates into him; not only pain and suffering, but the horror of evil itself. Just as people have the power of transmitting good to each other, they also have the power of transmitting evil. One can transmit evil to another human being by flattery, or by handing out pleasures and material comforts; but most often people transmit evil to others by doing harm to them.

Eternal Wisdom, however, does not leave the human soul entirely at the mercy of accidental events and the will of men. The evil inflicted from the outside on a human being in the form of a wound incites the desire for good and raises up automatically the possibility of a cure. When the wound has penetrated deeply, the desired good is the perfectly pure good. The part of the soul that asks, "Why has someone done evil to me?," is the deep part of the soul that dwells intact and perfectly innocent in every human being, including the most despoiled, from earliest childhood.

To preserve justice, to protect human beings from all evil, is above all to ensure that no one does evil to them. For those to whom evil has been done, it is to efface its material consequences by putting the victims into a situation where the wound, if it has not pierced too deeply, might be healed naturally by their welfare being taken care of. But for those in whom the wound has destroyed the soul, it is above all a matter of calming the thirst in them by giving them something to drink from the perfectly pure good.

There can be an obligation to inflict hurt in order to evoke this thirst so that it can be filled. This is what punishment is about. Those who have made themselves strangers to goodness to the point of looking for ways of increasing the evil around them cannot be reintegrated into goodness except by the infliction of harm. It is necessary to inflict this on them up to the point where the perfectly innocent voice in their depths says with astonishment, "Why is someone doing evil to me?" It is necessary that this innocent part of the soul of a criminal receive nourishment and that it grow until there is finally in its interior a judge for past crimes, in order that they might be condemned, and then, with the help of grace, so that they might be forgiven. The work of punishment is then done; the guilty is reintegrated into goodness, and ought to be publicly and solemnly reintegrated into the city.

Punishment is nothing else than this. Even capital punishment, though it excludes reintegration into the city in any literal sense, should not be anything else. Punishment is uniquely a procedure for giving pure good to those who do not want it; the art of punishing is the art of evoking in criminals the desire for pure good by pain, and even by death.

But we have entirely lost the concept of punishment. We no longer know that it consists in providing goodness. For us, it stops at inflicting hurt. This is why there is one thing, and one only in modern society that is more hideous than crime, and that is justice as a deterrent.

To take the idea of justice as a deterrent as the central motive in the war effort and in revolution is more dangerous than anyone might imagine. It is necessary to use fear in order to lessen the criminal activity of cowards; but it is appalling to make repressive justice, as we ignorantly think of it today, the motive of heroes.

Every time that someone today speaks of punishments, penalties, of retribution, of justice in the punitive sense, it is solely a question of the basest vengeance.

We think so little of this treasure of suffering and violent death that Christ took on himself and that he offers so often to those he loves that we throw it at those beings who are the most vile in our eyes, knowing that they will make no use of it. We have no intention of helping them make use of it.

For criminals, true punishment; for the afflicted for whom affliction has bitten into the bottom of their souls, a help capable of leading them to supernatural springs to quench their thirst; for everybody else, a life of well-being, including much beauty, and protection against those who would do them harm; everywhere a rigorous limitation to the tumult of lies, propaganda, and opinions; the establishment of a silence where the truth can sprout and grow. These things are what are due to human beings.

In order to assure that human beings get these things, one can only count on those people who have passed to the other side of a certain limit. Someone might object that there are not many of them. They are probably rare, but they cannot be counted anyhow; most of them are hidden. The pure good is only sent from heaven to us below in imperceptible quantities, whether it is in individual souls or in society. "The mustard seed is the smallest of all seeds." Persephone ate only one pomegranate seed. A pearl buried in a field is not visible. One can also note the leaven that is mixed with the dough.

But just as in chemical reactions of catalysts and bacteria, of which leaven is an example, so, too, in human things — the imperceptible grains of pure good operate in a decisive way by their mere presence, as long as they are put in the right place.

How does one put them there?

Much can be accomplished if among those who are in charge of showing to the public what things are worthy of praise, of admiration, of hope, of investigation, of inquiry, that at least some of them resolve in their hearts to scorn absolutely and without exception everything that is not pure goodness, perfect, true, just, and loving.

Above all it will happen if those who today hold onto the fragments of spiritual authority feel the obligation of never proposing anything for human aspiration other than goodness that is real and perfectly pure.

When we speak of the power of words, it is always a question of an illusory power and of error. But, by the effect of a providential disposition, there are certain words that, if one makes good use of them, have in themselves the virtue of illumining and raising us towards the good. These are words to which corresponds a perfection that is absolute and ungraspable by us. The virtue of illumination and of giving us traction towards the higher resides in these words themselves, in these words as they are, not in any conception we have of them. In order to make good use of them, they are not to be given any corresponding conception. What they express is inconceivable.

God and truth are such words. So, too, are justice, love, and good.

It is dangerous to use such words. Their usage is a trial. In order that a legitimate use be made of them, it is necessary at one and the same time both not to enclose them within any human conception and to join them with conceptions and actions that have been directly and exclusively inspired by their light. Otherwise, they quickly are recognized by everybody as being lies.

They are discomforting companions. Words such as "rights," "democracy," and "person" are more comfortable and are naturally preferable in the eyes of those who have assumed public functions, despite their good intentions. Public functions have no other significance than the possibility of doing good to human beings, and those who assume such functions with good intentions do want to spread good over their neighbors. But, they generally commit the mistake of believing that they can buy it on the cheap.

Words of the middle region—rights, democracy, person—have a proper use in their own region, which is the region of middle institutions. The inspiration from which all institutions proceed, of which all institutions are the outworkings, needs another language.

The relative subordination of the person to the collective is in the nature of things like that of the gram to the kilogram on a balance. But a balance can be set up so that a kilogram is tipped by a gram. One of the arms just needs to be a thousand times longer than the other one. The law of equilibrium rules over the inequality of weights. But an inferior weight will never tip the scales on a superior one unless their relations are established by the law of equilibrium.

In the same way, the person cannot be protected against the collective, and democracy secured, except by a crystallization in public life of the superior good, which is impersonal and without relation to any particular political form.

The word "person," it is true, is often applied to God. But in the passage where Christ proposes God to human beings as the model of the perfection that they are commanded to accomplish, he does not link it to an image of the personal, but to one that is impersonal: "Become children of your Father who is in heaven, and who makes his sun rise on the evil as well as the good, and who makes his rain fall on both the just and unjust."

This impersonal and divine order of the universe has as its images among us justice, truth, and beauty. Nothing less than these things is worthy of serving as inspiration for men who accept dying.

Above the institutions that are meant to protect rights, persons, and democratic liberties, it is necessary to invent other ones that are meant to discern and to abolish all that which, in contemporary life, buries souls under injustice, lies, and ugliness.

It is necessary to invent them, for they are unknown, and it is impossible to doubt that they are indispensable.

NOTES

1. For a detailed examination of the question, see Simone Fraisse, "Simone Weil, la personne et les droits de l'homme," *Cahiers Simone Weil* 7.2 (1984): 120–32, and Eric O. Springsted, "Beyond the Personal: Weil's Critique of Maritain," *Harvard Theological Review* 98.2 (2005): 209–18.

2. A literal translation of Weil's French translation of Blake. Blake's own verse: "Sooner murder an infant in its cradle than nurse unacted desires." Blake's verse in English can take a very different meaning than Weil gives it here. (Ed.)

CHAPTER SEVEN

The First Condition for the Work of a Free Person

(Condition première d'un travail non servile)

TRANSLATED BY LAWRENCE E. SCHMIDT

This article was written towards the end of Weil's time in Marseille, sometime in the late spring of 1942. Signed under the pseudonym "Emile Novis" (an anagram of "Simone Weil"), it was originally intended for the journal *Économie et humanisme*, but it did not appear until 1947, in *Le Cheval de Troie*, and then only in a truncated form. It is an admirable connection of Weil's anthropological considerations and her concerns about justice and labor, thus continuing her early work and looking forward to her final essays written during her last months in London.

There is in the work of human hands and, in general, in the skilled performance of a task, which is work properly understood, an irreducible element of servitude that even a perfectly just society cannot remove. This is because it is governed by necessity, not by finality. It is carried out because of a need, not in view of some good, "because one needs to earn one's living," as those who pass their days working say. One expends an effort at the end of which, as far as one can see, one will not have anything different from what one has now. Without this effort one would lose what one has.

But in human nature, there is no other source of energy for effort but desire. And it is not human nature to desire what one has. Desire is an orientation, the beginning of a movement towards something. The movement is towards a point where one is not. If the movement that has scarcely begun is fastened on the point of departure, one turns like a squirrel in a cage, like a condemned man in a cell. Turning around always produces discouragement quickly.

Discouragement, lassitude, disgust, is the great temptation of those who work, especially if they do so in inhuman conditions but even if they do not. At times, this temptation bites into the best of them, even more than the others.

To exist is not an end for a human being; it is only the ground on which all goods, true or false, stand. Goods are added to existence. When they disappear, when existence is no longer supplemented with any good, when it is naked, it no longer has any connection with the good. It is even an evil, which it is at the very moment when existence takes the place of all absent goods; then it becomes in itself the unique good, the only object of desire. The desire of the soul finds itself attached to a naked evil without any veil. The soul is then in a state of horror.

This horror is that of the moment when an imminent violence is going to inflict death. In the past, this moment of horror lasted a lifetime for the one who, unarmed under the sword of the winner of the fight, was spared. In exchange for the life that was left him, he had to exhaust his energy in efforts as a slave, all day long, every day, without anything to hope for except not being killed or whipped. He was no longer able to pursue any good but that of existing. The ancients used to say that on the day that one was made a slave one lost half one's soul.

But every condition in which one finds oneself necessarily in the same situation on the last day of a period of a month, of a year or of twenty years of effort as on the first day, has a resemblance to slavery. The resemblance is constituted by the impossibility of desiring anything other than what one has, of orienting one's effort towards the acquisition of a good. One makes an effort only to live.

The unit of time is thus the day. In this space, one turns round in circles. One moves back and forth between work and rest like a ball that is bounced from one wall to another. One works only because one needs to eat. But one eats in order to continue working. And again one works in order to eat.

Everything is an intermediary in this existence. Everything is a means. Finality is not grasped anywhere. The article made is a means; it will be sold. Who can put his being into it? The material, the tool, the body of the worker, his soul itself are means for fabrication. Necessity is everywhere, the good is nowhere.

It is not necessary to search far for the causes of the demoralization of the people. The cause is there; it is permanent; it is essential to the condition of work. It is necessary to look for the causes that in former times have prevented this demoralization from being produced.

A great moral inertia, a great physical force that makes effort almost unconscious, allows this emptiness to be supported. Otherwise, compensations are necessary. Ambition for another social condition for oneself or for one's children is one. Easy and violent pleasure is another that is of the same nature; it is the dream that takes the place of ambition. Sunday is the day on which one wants to forget that it is necessary to work. For that one must pay. One must be dressed as if one didn't work. Satisfactions for one's vanity and illusions of power that license procures very easily are required. Debauchery has exactly the same function as a drug; and the use of drugs is always a temptation for those who suffer. Finally, revolution is another compensation of the same nature. It is ambition translated into the collective, the crazy ambition of the ascent of all workers out of the workers' condition.

For most people, the revolutionary sentiment is in the first place a revolt against injustice, but it becomes quickly among many, as it has become historically, a worker imperialism entirely analogous to national imperialism. It has for its object entirely unlimited domination of a certain collectivity over all of humanity and over every aspect of human life. The absurd thing is that, in this dream, the domination would be in the hands of those who carry it out, and as a consequence cannot control it.

Insofar as it is a revolt against social injustice, the revolutionary idea is good and healthy. Insofar as it is a revolt against the essential evil of the workers' condition, it is a lie, because no revolution will wipe out this evil. But this lie has the greatest hold over people because this essential evil is resented more vigorously, more deeply, more sadly than injustice itself. Usually, moreover, they are confused. The name "opium of the people," which Marx applied to religion, belongs to religion when it betrays itself, but it is essentially applicable to revolution. The hope of revolution is always a drug.

Revolution satisfies at the same time this need for adventure, as being the thing the most opposed to necessity and that is another reaction against the same evil. The taste for novels and for police films and the tendency towards criminality that is seen among adolescents corresponds also to this need.

The bourgeoisie have been very naive in believing that a good recipe consisted in transferring to the people the end that governs their own life, that is to say, the acquisition of money. They have reached the farthest limit possible by piecework and the extension of exchange between the cities and the countryside. But they have done nothing but push dissatisfaction to a dangerous degree of exasperation. The cause of this is simple. Money, once it becomes the goal of desire and efforts, cannot tolerate in its domain internal conditions in which it is impossible to be enriched. A little industrialist, a little business man can become rich and become a big industrialist or a big business man. A teacher, a writer, a minister are rich or poor in any circumstance. But a worker who becomes very rich ceases being a worker, and it is almost always the same for a peasant. A worker cannot be bitten by the desire for money without desiring to leave, alone or with his comrades, the workers' condition.

The universe where the workers live has no finality. It is impossible for ends to enter there, except for brief periods that correspond to exceptional situations. The rapid fitting out of new countries, such as America or Russia, produces change upon change, at a rhythm that is so swift that it proposes to all, almost from day to day, new things to expect, to desire, to hope for; this feverish construction has been the great instrument of seduction for communist Russia, due to a coincidence, because it depends on the economic state of the country and not on a revolution or on Marxist doctrine. When metaphysical principles are elaborated, according to these exceptional circumstances that are passing and brief, as the Americans and Russians have done, these metaphysical principles are lies.

The family has as its end the raising of children. But unless one hopes for another condition for them—and in the nature of things such social movement is necessarily exceptional—the sight of children condemned to the same existence does not prevent one from feeling sorrow at the emptiness and heaviness of this existence.

This heavy emptiness causes a lot of suffering. It can be felt even by many of those whose culture is nonexistent and whose intelligence is weak. Those who, because of their state in life, do not know what it is, cannot judge fairly the actions of those who put up with it all their lives. It does not cause death, but it is perhaps as painful as hunger. Perhaps more so. Perhaps it would be literally true to say that bread is less necessary than the remedy for this pain.

There is no choice of remedies. There is only one. One thing alone makes the monotony bearable, that is a light from eternity; that is beauty.

There is only one case where human nature allows the desire of the soul to be carried not towards that which might be or which will be, but towards what exists now. This case is beauty. Everything that is beautiful is an object of desire, but one does not desire that it be different, one does not desire to change anything, one desires the very thing that exists. One looks with desire at the starry sky on a clear night and what one desires is exactly the sight that one has.

Since people are forced to place all their desire on what they already possess, beauty is made for them and they are made for beauty. Poetry is a luxury for the other social classes, but the common people need poetry like they need bread. And not only the poetry enclosed in words; by itself that cannot be of any use. They require that the daily substance of their lives be poetry itself.

Such poetry can only have one source. This source is God. This poetry can only be religion. By no trick, by no process, no reform, no upheaval, can finality enter into the universe where workers are placed by their very condition. But this universe can be completely linked to the only end that is true. It can be hooked onto God. The workers' condition is one where hunger for finality that constitutes the very being of every man cannot be satisfied except by God.

That is where their privilege lies. They are the only ones who can possess it. In every other condition, without exception, some particular ends are related to the activity. When it is a question of the salvation of one soul or many, there is no particular end that cannot make a screen and hide God. By detachment it is necessary to pierce through the screen. For the workers there is no screen. Nothing separates them from God. They only have to lift their heads.

The difficult thing for them is to lift their heads. Unlike other people, they have nothing beyond what is essential, nothing they must get rid of with effort. There is something that they lack. They are in need of intermediaries. When one has advised them to think about God and to make an offering to him of their troubles and their sufferings, one has still done nothing for them.

People go into churches expressly to pray; nevertheless, we know that they are unable to pray unless their attention is grasped by inter- mediaries that can keep them oriented towards God. The very architec- ture of the church, the images that it contains, the words of the liturgy and the prayers, the ritual gestures of the priest are these intermediaries. By paying attention to them, people are oriented towards God. How much greater then is the need for such intermediaries in the place of work, where one goes only to make a living. There everything binds one's thought to the earth.

But religious images cannot be placed there nor can it be suggested that the workers look at them. Neither can one propose that they recite prayers while working. The only objects of sense to which they can give their attention are matter, the instruments, and the gestures of their work. If these objects themselves are not transformed into mirrors of the light, it is impossible that during work their attention will be ori- ented towards the source of all light. There is no necessity more pressing than this transformation.

It is only possible if a reflecting property is found in matter as it is offered to the work of human beings. For it is not a question of fabri- cating fictions or arbitrary symbols. Fiction, imagination, dreams have nothing to do with what concerns the truth. But, fortunately for us, there is a reflecting property in matter. It is a mirror tarnished, clouded by our breath. It is only necessary to clean the mirror and to read the symbols that are written in matter from all eternity.

The Gospels contain some of them. In one's own room, in envision- ing a new and truthful birth, one must stop to think of the need for a moral death, and to read or repeat to oneself the words about a seed only bearing fruit by first dying. But he who is busy sowing seed can, if he wants, turn his attention to this truth without the aid of any word through his own gestures and the sight of the grain that is being buried in the ground. If he doesn't reason about it, if he just looks at it, the attention that he pays to the accomplishment of his task is not impeded but brought to the highest degree of intensity. Religious attention is not called the fullness of attention for nothing. Fullness of attention is nothing else but prayer.

It is the same for the separation of the soul and Christ that dries up the soul, just as the branch dries up when it is cut from the vine. The cutting of the vines takes days and days on large estates. But also there is a truth there that can be examined for days and days without being exhausted.

It would be easy to discover written from all eternity in the nature of things a lot of other symbols capable of transfiguring not only work in general but each task in its uniqueness. Christ is the brass serpent that one only has to gaze upon in order to escape death. But it is necessary to be able to look at it in a manner completely uninterrupted. For that reason it is necessary that the things that the needs and the obligations of life constrain us to watch reflect what they prevent us from watching directly. It would be very surprising if a church constructed by the hands of man should be full of symbols while the universe would not be infinitely full of them. They must be read.

The image of the cross compared to a balance in the Good Friday hymn could be an inexhaustible inspiration for those who carry loads or handle levers and are tired in the evening from the weight of things. In a balance, a considerable weight near the point of application can be lifted by a very light weight placed at a great distance. The body of Christ was a very light weight, but, because of the distance between the earth and the sky, it makes for a counterweight to the universe. In a manner infinitely different, but analogous enough to serve as an image, whoever is working, or lifting loads, or handling levers, should also make of his weak body a counterweight to the universe. It is too heavy, and often the universe makes the body and the soul bend with heaviness. But he who clings to the heavens will easily make a counterweight. Once a person has perceived this truth, he cannot be distracted by fatigue, boredom, or disgust. He can only be brought back to it.

The sun and the sap in the plants speak continually in the fields of what is the greatest thing in the world. We do not live by anything else but solar energy. We eat it, and it keeps us on our feet, it makes our muscles move, it operates bodily in all our acts. It is, perhaps under diverse forms, the only thing in the universe that constitutes a force opposed to gravity; it is what rises into the trees, what lifts loads through our arms, what drives our motors. It comes from an inaccessible source that we cannot approach even by one step. It comes down on us continually. But although it bathes us perpetually, we cannot capture it. Only the vegetable element of chlorophyll can capture it for us and make food out of it. It is only necessary that the earth be suitably managed by our efforts; then, through chlorophyll, solar energy becomes something solid and enters into us as bread, as wine, as oil, as fruits. The entire work of the peasant consists in caring for and serving this biological power that is a perfect image of Christ.

The laws of mechanics that derive from geometry and that apply to our machines contain supernatural truths. The oscillation of alternating motion is the image of our earthly condition. Everything that belongs to creatures is limited, except the desire in us that is the mark of our origin; and our covetousness that makes us seek the unlimited down here is the unique source of error and crime. The goods that things contain are finite, and so are the evils, and in general, a cause produces only a limited effect up to a certain point, beyond which, if it continues to act, the effect is reversed. It is God who imposes a limit on everything, and it is God by whom the sea is fettered. In God there is only one eternal act that, without change, is fastened on itself and has no other object but itself. In creatures there are only movements directed towards the outside, but which are forced to move back and forth by limit; this back-and-forth movement is a degraded reflection of the orientation towards oneself that is exclusively divine. This divine relationship has as an image in our machines, the relationship of circular movement and alternative movement. The circle is also the place of proportional means; in order to find in a perfectly rigorous manner the mean proportional between unity and a number that is not squared, there is no other method but to trace a circle. The numbers for which there exists no mediation that binds them naturally to unity are images of our misery; and the circle that comes from outside in a transcendent manner in relation to the sphere of numbers, to bring mediation, is the image of the unique remedy for this misery. These truths and many others are written in the simple sight of a pulley that establishes a back-and-forth movement. They can be read by someone with very elementary geometrical knowledge; the rhythm of work that corresponds with this oscillation makes them sensible to the body; a human life is a very short period to contemplate them.

Many other symbols could be found, some of them more intimately united to the very behavior of the one who is working. Sometimes it would be enough for the worker to extend to everything without exception his attitude with regard to work in order to possess the fullness of virtue. There are also some symbols to be found for those who have tasks to perform other than physical work. They can be found for the accountant in the elementary operations of arithmetic, for the cashiers in banking institutions, and so on. The reservoir is inexhaustible.

Beginning from there, one could do a great deal. One could transmit to adolescents these great images, allied to the notions of elementary science and general culture, in the circle of studies; or propose them as themes for their festivals, for their theatrical endeavors; or establish around them new festivals (for example, the vigil of the great day on which a little fourteen-year-old peasant works alone for the first time). One could see to it by these means that the men and women of the common people live bathed in an atmosphere of supernatural poetry, as in the Middle Ages, or even more than in the Middle Ages, for why should one limit oneself in one's ambition for the good?

In this way the feeling of intellectual inferiority that is so frequent and at times so sad for workers would be avoided, and also the arrogant self-confidence that replaces it after a superficial contact with the life of the mind. The intellectuals, for their part, would in this way be able to avoid at the same time the unjust disdain and the type of deference no less unjust that the crowd has made fashionable in our farm circles for some years now. Both would meet, without any inequality, at the highest point, that of the fullness of attention that is the fullness of prayer—at least those who would be able. The others would at least know that this point exists and would represent to themselves the diversity of ascending paths, which, while producing a separation at inferior levels, as does the thickness of a mountain, does not prevent equality.

School exercises have no other serious purpose than the formation of attention. Attention is the only faculty of the soul that grants access to God. School exercises use an inferior, discursive form of attention, the one that reasons; but, drawn on by a suitable method, it can prepare for the appearance in the soul of another type of attention, that which is the highest, intuitive attention. Intuitive attention in its purity is the unique source of perfectly beautiful art, of scientific discoveries that are truly luminous and new, of philosophy that truly moves towards wisdom, of love of the neighbor that is truly helpful; and when turned directly towards God, it constitutes true prayer.

In the same way as a symbol would allow one to dig and to mow while thinking about God, so a method that transforms school exercises in preparation for this superior type of attention would by itself permit an adolescent to think about God while he applied himself to a geometry problem or a Latin translation. Failing which, intellectual work, under a mask of liberty, is also for him a servile work.

Those who have some spare time need to exercise to the limit of their capacity the faculties of discursive intelligence in order to achieve intuitive attention; otherwise they become a hindrance. Especially for those who are forced by their social function to bring these faculties into play, there is without doubt no other way. But the hindrance is weak and the exercise can be reduced very much for those among whom the fatigue of a long workday almost entirely paralyses the faculties. For them, the same work that produces this paralysis, provided that it is transformed into poetry, is the way that leads to intuitive attention.

In our society, the difference in instruction more than the difference in wealth produces the illusion of social inequality. Marx, who is almost always at his strongest when he simply describes the evil, has legitimately branded as a degradation the separation of manual and intellectual work. But he did not realize that in every sphere, opposites have their unity in a transcendent plane in relation to each other. The point of unity of intellectual work and manual labor is contemplation, which is not work. In no society can the person who manages a machine exercise the same type of attention as the one who resolves a problem. But both can equally, if they desire it and if they have a method, promote the appearance and the development of another attention situated beyond all social obligation, and which constitutes a direct link with God, if each exercises the type of attention that constitutes his proper lot in society.

If students, young peasants, young workers represented to themselves in an entirely precise manner, as precise as the wheels of a mechanism clearly understood, the different social functions—insofar as they constituted equally efficacious preparation for the appearance in the soul of one identical transcendent faculty, which alone has value—equality would become a concrete thing. It would be then at the same time a principle of justice and of order.

The completely precise representation of the supernatural destiny of each social function alone gives a norm for our will to reform things. It alone permits one to define injustice. Otherwise, it is inevitable that one is deceived either by regarding as injustices some forms of suffering that are written in the nature of things, or by attributing to the human condition some forms of suffering that are the result of our crime, and fall on those who do not deserve them.

A certain subordination and a certain uniformity are forms of suffering included in the very essence of work and inseparable from the supernatural vocation that corresponds to it. They do not degrade a person. Everything that is added to them is unjust and does degrade. Everything that prevents poetry from crystallizing around these sufferings is a crime. For it is not enough to rediscover the lost source of such poetry; it is also necessary that the very circumstances of work permit it to exist. If they are evil, they kill it.

Everything that is indissolubly linked to the desire for, or fear of, change, or to the orientation of thought towards the future, should be excluded from any essentially changeless existence that simply needs to be accepted. In the first place, physical suffering, except for that which is made clearly inevitable by the necessity of work, for it is impossible to suffer without hoping for relief. Privations would be more in place in any other social condition than in this. Food, lodging, rest, and relaxation should be such that a workday taken by itself may normally be free of physical suffering. On the other hand, superabundance has no place in this life; for the desire for what is superfluous is itself unlimited and implies a change in condition. All advertising, all propaganda that is so varied in its forms, that arouses the desire for the superfluous in the countryside and among the workers, ought to be regarded as a crime.

An individual can always leave the workers' or the peasants' condition, either for basic lack of professional aptitude or because of the possession of different capabilities. But for those who are there, the only change that ought to be possible should be that of one's well-being as it is strictly related to the general well-being; there shouldn't be any reason to fear falling below or to hope reaching beyond this level. Security should be greater in this social condition than in any other. The chance events brought about by supply and demand should not be masters.

Human arbitrariness drives the soul to fear and hope, unless it can defend itself against it. It must be excluded, therefore, from work as much as possible. Authority should only be present when it can't be absent. Thus the small farm property is better than the large. It follows that wherever the small property is possible, the large is evil. In the same way, the production of machine-finished pieces in a small workshop is better than making them under the orders of a foreman. Job praises the death of whatever will allow the slave to no longer hear his master. Every time the voice that commands makes itself heard if a practical arrangement could substitute silence — there is evil.

But the worst outrage, the one that perhaps deserves to be likened to the crime against the Spirit, which cannot be forgiven, if it weren't committed by those unconscious of what they were doing, is the crime against the attention of the workers. It kills the faculty in the soul that is the very root of every supernatural vocation. The low quality of attention demanded by Taylorized work is not compatible with any other because it empties the soul of everything unconcerned with speed. This type of work cannot be transformed; it must be suppressed.

All the problems of technology and economy should be formulated functionally by conceiving of the best possible condition for the worker. Such a conception entails in the first place this standard: the entire society should be constituted in such a way that work does not drag down those who perform it.

It is not enough to want to spare them these forms of suffering; it would be necessary to want joy for them, not pleasures that are paid for, but joy that is free and that does not cast a slur on the spirit of poverty. The supernatural poetry, which ought to bathe their entire lives, ought also to be concentrated in a pure state, from time to time, in outstanding festivals. Festivals are as indispensable for this existence as the kilometer markers are to the comfort of the hiker. Free and demanding but diffi-cult trips like the Tour de France in other times should satisfy their hunger to see and to learn when they are young. Everything should be organized so that they lack nothing essential. The best among them should be able to possess in their life itself the fullness that the artisans seek indirectly through their art. If the vocation of the human being is to achieve pure joy through suffering, they are better placed than others to accomplish this in the most real way.

CHAPTER EIGHT

Literature and Morals

(*Morale et littérature*)

This article, signed with Weil's occasionally used pseudonym, "Emile Novis," was written in the fall of 1941 for *Cahiers du Sud*, but it was not published there until January 1944.

Nothing is so beautiful, marvelous, ever new, ever surprising, so full of sweet and continual delight, as the good. Nothing is so barren and dismal, monotonous and boring as evil. That is the way it is with real good and evil. Fictional good and evil are quite the opposite, though. Fictional good is boring and flat. Fictional evil is varied, interesting, attractive, profound, and seductive.

This is because in reality there is a necessity, like gravity, governing us that is missing in fiction. On a painter's canvas, but not in reality, you can paint anything. In the space that separates the sky and the earth, things fall effortlessly, indeed inevitably when there is nothing beneath them. They don't rise, or barely so, and only then with difficulty and by artificial means. A man coming down a ladder who misses a rung and falls, presents a sad and uninteresting spectacle, even if it is the first time we have seen such a thing. On the other hand, even if we saw it every day, we would never get tired of watching someone walking up to the clouds on air and then downwards, as if he were on a ladder. It is the same with pure good. A harsh necessity, quite like gravity, condemns humans to evil, forbidding them all good except a strictly limited good that is obtained only with difficulty, and that is mixed and soiled with evil. Except, that is, when the supernatural that suspends the effect of earthly necessity appears on earth. If, however, I paint someone rising through the air, that is of no interest. It is only interesting if the thing really exists. Unreality steals all value from the good.

A man who walks naturally is a banal and uninteresting sight. Men who jump around and leap bizarrely make me stop and amuse myself for a while by watching them. But if I were then to see that they were barefoot and trying to walk on coals, everything would change. The jumps, the leaps are then frightening, intolerable to watch, and, at the same time, through the horror, boring and monotonous. A man who walks naturally across the same coals, though, will arrest and hold my passionate interest. So it is that evil, insofar as it is fictional, draws its interest from the variety of forms that it takes, forms that spring from pure fantasy. The necessity inseparable from reality effaces this interest. The simplicity that makes fictional good a pallid thing that cannot get a glance from us is an unfathomable marvel in real good.

Since literature is above all a product of fictions, it would seem that immorality is inseparable from it. So it is wrong to reproach writers with being immoral, at least without reproaching them for being writers, as some courageous people in the seventeenth century did. Those who pretend to a high morality are no less immoral than anybody else; they're just worse writers. With them as with others, whenever they write, despite themselves, good is boring and evil is more or less attractive. On that account, one could condemn all literature *en bloc*. And why not? Writers and readers for their part will passionately cry out that immorality is not an aesthetic criterion. But here they need to prove, which they have never done, that one should apply only aesthetic criteria to literature. As readers do not constitute a unique species, as those who read are the same human beings who perform any number of other functions besides reading, it is impossible that literature should exempt itself from the categories of good and evil under which all human activities are subsumed. Every activity has two relations to good and evil—first, in its execution, and then in its principle. Thus a book, on the one hand, can be well or badly done, and, on the other hand, come from good or evil.

But it is not only in literature that fiction generates immorality. It does so, too, in life itself, for the substance of our life is made nearly entirely of fiction. We tell ourselves tales about our future. Without a heroic love of truth, we recount our past, all the while refashioning it to our taste. Not looking too closely at other people, we tell ourselves stories about what they think, what they are saying, what they are doing. Reality furnishes the elements of these stories, just as romantic novelists often take their plots from the news, but we wrap them in a fog of inverted values, inverted just as they are in all fiction, where evil attracts and good bores. It is only when reality gives us a strong enough shock that we wake up for a second, such as when we come close to a saint, or when we fall into the realms of affliction or crime. It is only in such cases, or similar ones, that, for a moment, we sense the horrible monotony of evil or the unfathomable marvel of goodness. But soon enough we fall back into the half-dream peopled by our narrational fancies.

Yet, something else also has the power of awakening us to the truth. This is the work of writers of genius, at least the work of those whose genius is of the first order and who have arrived at full maturity. These writers go beyond fiction, and they take us with them. Under the form of fiction, they give us something in writing that is equivalent to the depth of reality, the depth that life itself presents us with every day, even though we do not know how to grasp it because we are making ourselves feel good by lies.

Although the works of these writers are made up of words, the gravity that governs souls is nonetheless present in them. It is present, and it is front and center. Although this gravity is often sensed in our souls, it is disguised by the very effects that it produces. Submission to evil is always accompanied by errors and lies. Anyone swept down the slope of cruelty or fear cannot make out the nature of the force that is pushing her, much less the relations between this force and all the conditions of which it is a part. In the words put together by genius, several slopes are visible and sensible all at the same time, and related to each other as they really are, and the listener or reader does not have to fall down them himself to know them. He senses gravity here as someone who is safe and not subject to vertigo senses it when looking over a cliff. He discerns the unity and diversity of its forms in the architecture of the abyss. This is how both the slope of victory and the slope of defeat can both be manifest and simultaneously sensible in the *Iliad*. That is never the case for a soldier actually in combat. The plays of Aeschylus and Sophocles, certain ones of Shakespeare, Racine's *Phèdre*—alone among French tragedies—several comedies of Molière, the *Grand Testament* of Villon, enclose this gravity as genius alone can capture it. These poets had genius, and it was oriented to the good. There is also demonical genius and it, too, has its maturity. But although the maturity of genius is conformity to the true relation of good and evil, the work that corresponds to the maturity of demonical genius is silence. Rimbaud is both its best example and its symbol.

All writers who are not geniuses of the first order in their full maturity have as their unique reason for being the creation of a space where such genius might appear someday. This function alone justifies their existence, which otherwise ought to be outlawed because of the immorality to which they are condemned by the order of things. To reproach a writer with immorality is to reproach him with not being a genius, or one of the second rank—if that is not an oxymoron, or that his genius is not yet developed. If he has no genius, in one sense that is not his fault. In another, it is his one sin. To seek a remedy for the immorality of letters is an entirely vain enterprise. Genius is the only remedy, and accessing the source of genius is not within the reach of our efforts.

But what can and ought to be corrected, by the very consideration of this irremediable immorality, is letting writers usurp the function of spiritual direction, a function that is hardly suited to them. Only the geniuses of the first order in their full maturity have that aptitude. With respect to other writers, unless they have a philosophical vocation as well as their literary one, and that is rare, their conception of the world and of life, their opinions about the problems we have to deal with cannot be of any interest, and it is ridiculous to ask them about them. This usurpation began in the eighteenth century, above all in Romanticism. It introduced into literature a messianic puffery that is contrary to the purity of art. In an earlier age, writers were the domestic servants of great people. This position often meant they were in painful situations, but it was better than messianic delusion, not only with respect to the moral health of both writers and the public but with respect to art itself.

This usurpation has had its gravest possible effects only in the last half or quarter century, because it has been only since then that its influence has penetrated to the people. There has probably always been, more or less, bad oral and written literature circulating among the people. But in an earlier age, there was an antidote in the things of perfect beauty in which popular life was steeped, such as religious ceremonies, prayers, songs, folk tales, and dances. And above all literature then did not have any authority. In the last quarter century the mantle of authority that is linked to the function of spiritual direction, now usurped by writers, has fallen upon the worst sort of publications. There has been a continuum between this publishing and the highest literary production, and the public knew it. The same gentlemanly milieu where no one ever refused to shake another's hand contained those who occupied themselves exclusively with these publications, and their occasional contributors, and our greatest names. Between a Valéry poem and an advertisement for beauty cream promising a rich marriage to whoever uses it, at no point was there a rupture in continuity. Thus literature's spiritual usurpation has given a beauty cream advertisement as much authority in the eyes of little village girls as the words of priests. Is anyone surprised that we have fallen to where we are now? To have permitted that is a crime of which all those who know how to use a pen ought to bear the responsibility of remorse.

For centuries, spiritual direction was exclusively in the hands of priests. Often they exercised it atrociously, as is seen in the butchers of the Inquisition. But at least they had some claim to the job. In truth, only the greatest saints are really capable of it, as is the case with the greatest of writers of genius. But all priests by their profession witness to the saints, looking to them for inspiration, trying to follow and imitate them, and above all the one true saint, Christ. Where they do not do this, which often happens, they fail in their duty. For the few who do this, they communicate more good than they possess in themselves. What comes from a writer on the contrary comes only from within himself. He can be subject to the influence of other writers, but he cannot draw his inspiration from them.

When priests had lost nearly all of this function of spiritual direction because of the effect of the Enlightenment, writers and savants took over their place. In both cases, the absurdity is the same. Mathematics, physics, biology are just as foreign to spiritual direction as the art of word mongering is. When literature and science usurp this function, there is no longer any spiritual life. Today, numerous signs would seem to indicate that this usurpation of writers and savants has come to an end, although its appearance lingers. That would be cause for joy, if one were not afraid that something surely worse will take its place.

But the works of authentic geniuses of past centuries remain. They are still with us. Contemplating them is the inexhaustible source of an inspiration that can legitimately direct us. For this inspiration, for those who know how to receive it, tends, as Plato said, to give wings that can push against gravity.

Emile Novis

CHAPTER NINE

The Responsibilities of Literature

(Lettre aux Cahiers du Sud *sur les responsabilités de la littérature)*

Cahiers du Sud had published in October 1940 and March 1941 two articles seeking to refute the then oft-trumpeted notion that writers had contributed to France's defeat in 1940 by lowering its sense of morals and hence its strength. Weil, who was at this time deeply concerned with questions of value, weighed in on the controversy in her own distinctive way with this letter in 1941. However, the journal did not publish it until 1951.

Reading the allusion made by Gros to the controversy over the responsibility of writers, I cannot help but return to this question in order to defend a way of looking at it that is contrary to the view of this journal, and contrary to nearly everyone to whom I am sympathetic, and that appears, unfortunately, like the views of those with whom I do not have any sympathy.

I believe that writers of the present time are responsible for the misfortune of our time. By that, I do not mean just the defeat of France; the affliction of our times goes farther than that. It extends to the whole world—to Europe, to America, and to other continents wherever Western influence has penetrated.

It is true, as Mauriac said, that the best contemporary books are hardly read. But the responsibility of writers cannot be measured by circulation figures. For the prestige of literature is immense. One can see that in the earlier efforts made by certain political movements to enlist the names of celebrated writers in the causes of their demagoguery. Even people to whom those names are unknown are not any less susceptible to the prestige of the literature that they ignore. People have never read as much as they read today. They do not read books, but they do read mediocre and bad magazines; these magazines are everywhere—in the villages, in the suburbs. So, by virtue of the effect of the literary habits of our time, the worst of these magazines and the best of our writers form a seamless whole. This fact, which is known, or, rather, confusedly sensed by the public, keeps it from seeing the ignobility of publicity pitches, which borrow the prestige of high literature. There has been, in the course of the last few years, unbelievable baseness, such as love advice dished out by famous writers. Surely not everybody degrades himself in this way, not by any means. But those who do have not been disavowed or pushed away by the others; they do not lose the respect of their peers. This easiness of literary habits, this tolerance of lowness, gives to our most eminent writers a responsibility for demoralizing country girls who have never left their villages and who have never heard of these famous names.

But writers have an even more direct responsibility.

The essential character of the first half of the twentieth century is the weakening and near disappearance of the concept of value. This is one of those rare phenomena that seems to be, as far as anyone can tell, something truly new in human history. It could have happened before, of course, in the course of some period that has vanished into oblivion, as could become the case with our time. This phenomenon has been seen in many areas outside literature, indeed, in all of them. The substitution of quantity for quality in industrial production, the discredit into which skilled labor has fallen among workers, the substitution of diplomas for culture as the goal of studies among students are expressions of it. Even science itself no longer has any criterion of value since the demise of classical science. But writers used to be the guardians par excellence of the treasure that has been lost, and a number of them are now proud of the loss.

Dadaism and surrealism are extreme cases of this. They have given expression to the intoxication of total license, an intoxication into which the mind is plunged when, rejecting any consideration of value, it gives itself over to immediacy. The good is the pole towards which the human mind necessarily orients itself, not only in its actions but in every sort of effort, including pure thinking. The surrealists erected a model of unoriented thought; they chose for their supreme value the total absence of value. License has always intoxicated human beings, and that is why, throughout history, towns have been sacked. But the sack of villages has not always had a literary equivalent. It has it now in surrealism.

Other writers of the same period and the one just before it have not gone quite so far, but nearly all—excepting three or four—are more or less affected by the same indifference, the indifference to the sense of value. Words such as spontaneity, sincerity, gratuitousness, richness, enrichment, words that all imply a nearly complete indifference to the opposing poles that value vibrates between, flow from their pens more often than words that are within the moral space of good and evil. Moreover, this last type of words when they are used have been degraded, especially those having to do with the good, as Valéry remarked some years ago. Words such as virtue, nobleness, honor, honesty, and generosity have nearly all become words that are difficult to use, or they have taken on a bastard sense. Language does not give us any other resources to praise a person's character. There are a few more, but not many, to praise a person's mind: but mind itself, and words having to do with intelligence, the intelligent, and others like them have also been degraded. What has happened to words renders sensible the progressive vanishing of the concept of value, and even though this fate of words does not depend on writers, one cannot help but hold them particularly responsible, since words are their job.

Bergson's work has been justly praised in our time, and his influence on present thought and literature has been often noted. Yet, at the center of the philosophy from whence come his three primary works is found a concept that is essentially foreign to any consideration of value, which is to say, the notion of Life. It is indeed in vain that one would want to use his philosophy as a base for Catholicism, which does not have any need for it anyhow, since it possesses much more ancient bases. The work of Proust is filled with analyses that seek to describe nonoriented states of the soul; the good appears in them only in rare moments when either by the effects of memory or beauty, eternity allows itself to be present through time. One can make similar remarks on most writers before, and above all after, 1914. In a general way the literature of the twentieth century is essentially psychological. Yet, the psychological consists in describing states of the soul while flattening them all out on the same plane without concern for value, as if good and evil were external to them, as if the effort towards the good could be absent at any moment from the thought of a human being.

Writers do not have to be professors of morals, but they do have to give expression to the human condition. For nothing is so essential to human life, for all people and at every moment, as good and evil. When literature becomes deliberately indifferent to the opposition of good and evil, it betrays its function and has no pretense to excellence. Racine mocked the Jansenists when he was young, but he did not mock them when he wrote *Phèdre*, and *Phèdre* is his masterpiece. From this point of view, it is not true that there is a continuity in French literature. It is not true that Rimbaud and his successors (setting aside some passages of *A Season in Hell*) were the continuation of Villon. What did it matter that Villon stole? The act of stealing was, for his part, perhaps a matter of necessity, perhaps it was a sin, but it was not a matter of thrill seeking or gratuitousness. The sense of good and evil impregnates all his verses, just as it impregnates all work that does not see human destiny as foreign.

To be sure, there is something even more foreign to good and evil than amorality, and that is a certain kind of morality. Those who are currently putting the blame on famous writers are worth infinitely less than they, and the "moral reorientation" that certain people would like to impose would be much worse than the state of things that they are pretending to remedy. If our present suffering ever does lead to a moral reorientation, it will not be accomplished by slogans, but in silence and moral solitude, through pain, misery, terror, in the deepest part of each spirit.

Simone Weil

CHAPTER TEN

At the Price of an Infinite Error

The Scientific Image, Ancient and Modern

(*La science et nous*)

This extensive essay was written in the spring of 1941. It appears that it was prompted by the publication of a book by
Max Planck in the beginning of the year, namely, in French
translation, *Initiations à la physique*. The essay was never finished, as other work came to occupy Weil's attention. Nevertheless, the essay is a very full one. Not only does it contain
Weil's reflections on modern science, but it seeks to relate it to
Greek thought, which was of paramount importance to her. It
also shows numerous bridges between and among her philosophical, religious, anthropological, and cultural thinking. By
itself, its chief significance is probably less in its criticism of
quantum theory, which would not disturb physicists, and more
in its concerns about how as thinkers we represent and think
the world in which we live. The text as presented here contains
several pages not originally in the first French edition of this
essay in *Sur la science* or in the previous English translation,
"Classical Science and After," in *On Science, Necessity, and the
Love of God*.

Something happened to the people of the Western world at the beginning of the century, something quite strange: we lost science without
even being aware of it, or at least, what had been called science for the

last four centuries. What we now have under this name is something else, something radically different, and we do not know what it is. Probably no one knows what it is. The public at large noticed something singular around 1920 in relation to Einstein and were full of admiration, for is it not fortunate that our century is admirable? But the theory of relativity had nothing to revolutionize, since around 1900 quantum theory had already done that. Moreover, although we find bizarre the applications of non-Euclidean geometry, the curvature of space, time considered as a dimension, velocity that is both infinite and measurable, the idea that motion and rest have sense only in relation to a frame of reference, which is Einstein's theory, in none of this is there anything new or strange; it is already in Descartes, and even if Newton disputed it, there was no evident absurdity in it. It is quite a different matter with respect to quanta of energy.

Quantum theory marks a rupture in the evolution of science in two ways. First, it marks the return of the discontinuous. Number, as far as we know, was initially the only object to which mathematical method was applied; its study had advanced so far that a Babylonian adolescent four thousand years ago knew as much algebra as a French *lycée* student does today, but this algebra consisted of numeric equations. Moreover, the way that certain problems were presented—one of them speaks of a sum of two numbers of which one is a number of days, and the other a number of workers—seems to indicate that algebra was at that time what it is today to certain minds, that is, a manipulation of relations of purely conventional designations that were not considered to be knowledge of the world as such; the world never furnishes us such given facts.

As far as we can tell, it was in Greece in the sixth century BC that mathematical method left off being concerned with numbers alone and was applied to the world, and it did so by taking the continuous as its object. That this change of object was a conscious choice by the Greeks, we have as evidence the fact that until a much later time, that of Diophantus, they always pretended to be ignorant of algebra and its equations; they only admitted algebraic relations when dressed as geometric propositions. The *Epinomis* defines geometry as "an assimilation of numbers naturally unlike each other, an assimilation that is made evident thanks to the properties of plane figures"; this is to define quantity, expressible or not, in numbers and fractions. The expression "like or similar numbers" seems to indicate that the constructions of similar triangles, the base of geometry, constituted for the Greeks a method to discover proportions, and without doubt the construction of the right-angled triangle, the combination of similar triangles, a method to discover mean proportionals. Proportion was perhaps for the Greeks the motivating force of their geometrical discoveries, for the greater part of their discoveries could be arranged around two problems, namely, the search for a mean proportional between two numbers, and the search for two mean proportionals between two numbers. Plato pushed to solve the second and could not help but continually celebrate the solution of the first with a singular exaltation.

Be that as it may, the Greeks at the beginning of the fourth century BC possessed the complete theory of real numbers,[1] in its most rigorous form, and a perfectly precise conception of the integral calculus. As the lines represented by geometrical figures are always at the same time trajectories of motion, their geometry constituted for them the science of nature; "God is a perpetual geometer." For the Babylonian algebraic equation the notion of function was substituted, the soul of all scientific knowledge. Using letters to represent, not just whole numbers or fractions, but numbers in the sense of real numbers, allowed the Renaissance to conserve not only the heritage of the Greeks but that of the Babylonians as transmitted through Diophantus, the Hindus, the Arabs; the form of the equation served to express the function; the differential and integral calculus followed immediately from that; and the algebra created by the Renaissance, a modern equivalent of Greek geometry, and expressing like it combinations of continuous magnitudes analogous to distances, played the same instrumental role for knowing nature. Fourier's series for heat is a brilliant example of it.

But the human mind cannot stand on either number or the continuous exclusively; it moves from one to the other, and something in nature corresponds to each of them, without which we, as we exist, we who always think in terms of numbers and of space, cannot live. In the course of the nineteenth century, and especially towards its end, the discontinuous imposed itself anew on scientific thought in all its branches. In mathematics: group theory and everything that proceeds from it, the extension of arithmetic and its new relations with analysis; in physics: atoms, the kinetic theory of gases, quanta; all chemical laws;

in biology, mutations; all of these are signs of the return of the discontinuous in science. This return, a step in the inevitable balancing of two correlative notions, is entirely natural; what is, without exaggeration, contrary to nature is the use of the discontinuous in contemporary physics, that is, when one divides energy into packets, whereas energy is nothing other than a function of space. By that reasoning, what was called science in 1900, and what we now call today "classical science," has disappeared, because we have radically suppressed what it meant.

From the Renaissance up to the end of the nineteenth century, scientists were not simply accumulating experiments; they had a goal in mind; they were pursuing a representation of the universe. The model for this representation was work, or, more exactly, the elementary, crude form of work, that work in which practice, know-how, skill, and inspiration have no role, the work of labor, the work of one's hands. Between desire and its satisfaction there is for us a distance that, in one sense, is the world itself. If I desire to see a book on the table that is currently on the floor, I will not be satisfied until I have grasped the book and lifted it the whole distance that separates the table from the floor. If one considers a horizontal plane placed between that of the table and that of the floor, no matter what happens among the infinity of possibilities, the book will never end up on the table without having traversed this plane. I can spare myself the weight of the book by tearing each page out, one by one, and lifting only a page at a time; but I will have to do it over again as many times as there are pages in the book. One can imagine in my place an idiot, a criminal, a hero, a sage, a saint, it does not make any difference. The set of geometric and mechanical necessities to which such action always has to submit constitutes the original curse by which Adam was punished, and it is what makes the difference between this universe and a terrestrial paradise, namely, the curse of work.

Classical science, which the Renaissance revived and which then perished around 1900, tried to represent all phenomena in the universe, by imagining for any two successive states of a system established by observation, as intermediaries that were analogous to those through which a man executing simple work would pass. It thought of the universe on a model of the relation between some human action and the necessities that were its obstacles and that imposed conditions on it. There was no question, to be sure, of imagining some kind of will at work behind the phenomena of nature, for such a will would not be analogous to the human will, as it would not be linked to the body, and it would be supernatural, which is to say that it could dispense with the conditions of work. Thus, in order to establish an analogy between the phenomena of nature and work, it was necessary to eliminate from work one of the two terms that define it and without which it cannot be conceived. It is true, the law of work that rules human life is the law of indirect action by which each step of execution is independent of the previous one and the one to come, indifferent to desire and to a hoped-for result; if I want to lift a very heavy stone, I will succeed not by lifting it but in lowering something, if that something is a lever. Through such a chain of intermediaries to which my desire is external, I touch the world, and I think of the world on the model of a chain of intermediaries, pure intermediaries that are intermediary to nothing. At least I try to think of it in this way. But I cannot succeed entirely in imagining work without a worker. I cannot conceive of an obstacle that is not opposed to any action. I cannot think of conditions that are not the conditions of any given project. This is why there is found an impenetrable obscurity—one can convince oneself of it just by perusing a textbook—in the simple and fundamental notions of mechanics and physics, that is, rest, motion, velocity, acceleration, mass at a point, system of bodies, inertia, force, work, energy, potential.

Nevertheless, classical science came in the end to subsume all study of natural phenomena under a single concept, directly derived from that of work, namely, the notion of energy. This was the result of long effort. Lagrange, building upon the discoveries of the Bernoullis, d'Alembert, and by means of the differential calculus, came to define by a unique formula all possible states of equilibrium or of motion of any system of bodies under any forces—or, what amounts to the same thing, to masses and velocities—that is to say, on something analogous to weight; from that Maxwell, in a flash of genius, concluded that if one can imagine a mechanical model for just one phenomenon, one can do so for an infinity of them. It is to understand that the explanatory value is the same in every case. Hence it is pointless to imagine even one of them; it suffices to establish that it is possible to imagine the model at all. The notion of energy, which is a function of distance and force, or even of mass and velocity, is the common measure of all work, that is to say, of all transformations analogous to the lifting or falling of a weight, by furnishing the mean; the unique formula of dynamics says that from one state of a system to another, the variation of this function is zero if no force exterior to this system intervenes. To apply such a formula to a phenomenon is to establish that it is possible to imagine a mechanical model for this phenomenon. Thus one does not have to worry anymore about intermediaries, one can simply suppose that the relation between the successive states experimentally observed of a system is identical or equivalent to the relation between the beginning and end points of a human work; and for each type of phenomenon one seeks to establish numerical equivalences between certain measures taken during the course of experiments, on the one hand, and, on the other, the distances and weights that constitute for a human the obstacles to one's work. The idea of work is always present, since energy is always measured in distances and weights; and though the force may be a function of mass and acceleration, and not something like an effort, the place held by acceleration in the formulas comes from the constraint of weight on all human action. Nineteenth-century science consisted of determining in several types of phenomena numerical equivalences with distances and weights, as Joule first did for heat.

Science did something else also. It invented a new concept by translating, in order to apply it to energy, the necessity that, with work, weighs most heavily upon human life. This necessity belongs to time itself and consists in the fact that time has a direction, in that the sense of a transformation is never indifferent to where it starts and where it ends up. We experience this necessity, not only by the aging that slowly grasps us in its embrace and that undoes us, but also by the happenings of each day. It only takes a moment and a minor effort to throw a book off the table, mix up a pile of papers, stain some clothing, crumple some linen, burn a field of wheat, or kill a man. It takes considerable effort to put a book up on the table, put papers in order, clean clothing, iron linen; a year of pain and toil is needed to get a new harvest out of the field; one cannot make a dead man come back to life, and to raise a child to adulthood takes twenty years. This necessity that constrains us so strictly is reflected in social constraint, by the power that it gives to those who know how to burn fields and kill men, things over in a second, over those who know how to grow wheat and to raise children, which are slow things. Space cannot in any way express this necessity because it is indifferent to all directions. Weight also does not express it, since the weights in dynamics are elastic and never fall without rebounding; it is necessary that they do so in order to express the essential necessity of human work, transported by the physicist into nature, which is to say, that nothing in the world is exempt from it. But beyond that it is necessary to add something to the notion of energy, defined by distances and weights, in order to express the condition of all human action. It is necessary to add that all transformations have a sense to them that is not indifferent. But it is necessary to say it in an algebraic formula, in the language of mathematics applied to physics. Clausius discovered it and thus invented what is called entropy.

One assumes in every phenomenon that there is a transformation of energy such that there cannot be found any way, once the transformation has taken place, of reestablishing the initial state throughout. One enacts this principle by the fiction of a quantity that, in every system in which a change has taken place, always increases, except in the case of intervening external factors; the sole exceptions being purely mechanical phenomena, not accompanied by changes in heating or cooling, but there are no such things. The search for an algebraic formula for this quantity is the most complete triumph of the notion of limit, earlier found by Eudoxus at the same time as the integral calculus; for it is only a question of limits. Since it is a question of variations linked to those of heat, one looks for a case, which is impossible, where a phenomenon is produced without there being any addition or loss of heat, and where nevertheless temperature plays a role, which is impossible; yet, despite this, a case is furnished by perfect gases, gases that do not exist, but that, unlike those that do, can expand without changing temperature, and by an infinitely slow compression through a pressure equal to that of the gas, which again is obviously impossible; by equating a differential formula to zero and then by integrating, one finds a function of temperature and volume, which, because it is constant, corresponds by hypothesis to entropy. The increase of entropy is a function of the increase of energy, of the increase of volume, of pressure, of temperature, and of mass; or again, it is proportional to the mass and to the ratio of the heat given to the temperature. Other calculations permit one to apply the notion of entropy to gases that do exist. Such was the crowning achievement of classical science, which led everyone to believe that it would be possible by calculations, measurements, numerical equivalents to read across all phenomena that occur in the universe simple variations of energy and entropy conforming to a simple law. The thought of succeeding at that was what inspired minds. The catastrophe came soon after.

The importance of this four-century enterprise cannot be denied. The necessity that constrains us in the simplest actions gives us, whenever we relate it to things, the idea of a world so completely indifferent to our desires that we have the experience of being pretty much nothing. In thinking of ourselves from the point of view of the world, if one can put it this way, we arrive at this cosmic indifference then with respect to ourselves; without it, we cannot be delivered from desire, from hope, from fear, from duty, and without it there is neither virtue nor wisdom, and we live in a dream. The contact with necessity is that which substitutes reality for our dreams. An eclipse is a nightmare when one does not understand that the disappearance of the sun in an eclipse is analogous to the disappearance of the sun for anyone covering his eyes with his coat; when one understands it, the eclipse is simply a fact. Some splendid verses of Lucretius give the sense of what is purifying in the sight and experience of necessity; affliction thus endured is a purification of this type, as is classical science also a purification, if one can make good use of it, for it tries to read through all appearances this inexorable necessity that makes of the world, a world where we do not count, a world where we work, a world indifferent to desire, to aspirations, and to the good; it is the study of the sun that shines indifferently on the just and the unjust.

But one cannot regret that it came to an end, for it was by its very nature limited. Its interest is limited and even weak; it is terribly monotonous, and once one has gotten down its principle, that is to say, the analogy between events in the world and the simplest form of human work, it reveals nothing new, it just accumulates discoveries. The discoveries do not give any new value to the principle; they draw their value from it. Or if it takes from them even greater value, it is only insofar as, when at the moment of discovery, it is genuinely grasped by a human mind, for the act by which a mind suddenly comes to read necessity through appearances is always of value; as Fresnel read necessity in the fringes of light and darkness by an analogy with the waves in water. In the same way, the attitude of the scientific mind is admirable at the moment when it is held by someone who is gripped by events, dangers, responsibilities, emotion, maybe even terrors, as, for example, when one is on a sailing vessel or airplane. In hindsight, nothing is so dismal, so barren as the accumulation of scientific results that constitute, in books, a state of dead residue. The accumulation of a set of works of classical physics without number is not to be desired.

It is not possible, anyhow; classical science is limited in how far it can go, because the human mind is limited. Men differ from each other; but even with respect to the most gifted, the human mind cannot embrace an unlimited number of facts clearly conceived; moreover, a synthesis of them can only be conceived by a single mind; there cannot be a synthesis between a fact thought by me and a fact thought by my neighbor, so as long as we each remain thinking silently to ourselves, "two," there will never be a four. For all physical theory is a synthesis whose elements are facts conceived as analogous to each other. As facts are accumulated by generations of succeeding scientists, as long as there is not any growth in the capacity of the human mind, the quantity of facts to be grasped will in the end exceed by far what the human mind can bear; the scientist has hence in mind no more facts, but only syntheses made by others from the facts, syntheses of which he will in his own turn make yet another synthesis without having revised those facts. This operation has less value, less interest, and fewer chances of succeeding, the greater the distance between the thought and the facts on which it is based. Thus classical science contained in its progress a progressive paralyzing factor that was one day going to kill it.

But even when it might embrace the entire universe and all its phenomena, classical science was still going to be limited; it could only give a partial account of the universe. The universe it described is the universe of the slave, and the human, although it includes slaves, is not only a slave. The human is indeed this being who seeing an object on the floor and wanting to see it on the table is constrained to lift it; but the human being is also, at the same time, something else. The world is indeed the world that puts a distance that is hard to cross between all desire and all accomplishment, but it is also, at the same time, something else. We are confident that it is something else; otherwise we could not exist. It is true that the matter that constitutes the world is a tissue of blind necessities, absolutely indifferent to our desires; it is true also, in a sense, that it is absolutely indifferent to the aspirations of the human spirit, indifferent to the good; but in another sense that is not true. For if there has ever been in the world true sanctity, even if it were just in one person for one day, then there is a sense in which sanctity is something of which matter is capable; since matter alone and that which is inscribed in matter exists. The body of a human being, and consequently the body of a saint, is nothing other than matter, and it is a piece of this world, of the same world that is a tissue of mechanical necessities. We are ruled by a double law; an evident indifference and a mysterious complicity of the matter that constitutes the world with respect to the good; remembering this double law is that which strikes our heart in the sight of beauty.

Nothing is more foreign to the good than classical science, which takes the most elementary form of work, the work of a slave, as the principle for reconstructing the world; the good is never invoked, even by way of contrast, or as an opposing term. One can perhaps explain why it is that in other times and places, excepting the course of the last four centuries in this little peninsula of Europe and its American extension, that people did not go to the trouble of elaborating a positive science. They wanted more to seize upon the secret complicity of the universe with the good. There is a great attraction in that, but also a great danger; for human beings easily confound the aspiration to the good with desire itself; sin is nothing other than this bastard mixture; thus, in trying to seize in the world values rather than necessity, one risks encouraging in himself what is troublesome. But if one can avoid this danger, such an attempt is perhaps a method of purification that is quite superior to that of positive science. To be sure, it cannot result in a communicable sort of knowledge like science; one will be convinced of that if he reflects on the fact that all scientific study of natural phenomena, as abstract as it may be, is to arrive at, at the end of the day, a collection of technical recipes, while sages, great artists, and saints never make use of a recipe, not only for others, but even for their own use, although they each do have a method of giving existence to the good to which they aspire. The results accomplished by efforts to think the universe, the human body, the human condition, all in their relation to the good cannot perhaps be expressed in any language other than myth, or poetry, or in images; images not only made from words, but also from objects and actions. The choice of images can, to be sure, be more or less felicitous. But when it is a happy choice, the image always encloses some mystery in itself. The ordeals of the Middle Ages, for example, are images of this type—the fire that does not burn, the water that will not drown the innocent—clear, although very crude. In the same epoch, alchemy is a mysterious image and more elevated; it is, indeed, wrong to take alchemists as the precursors of today's chemists, since they regarded the most pure virtue and wisdom as an indispensable condition to the success of their operations. Lavoisier, for his part, sought to combine oxygen and hydrogen in water by a foolproof recipe, one that indeed an idiot or criminal could succeed at as well as he himself. All other civilizations, except modern Europe, consist essentially in the working out of images of this type.

Among all the seeking for knowledge that there has been, excepting positive science, Greek science, despite its marvelous and unequaled clarity, is for us a mystery. In one sense, it is the beginning of positive science; and at first looking at it, the armed destruction of Greece seemed to be only an interruption of seventeen centuries, not a change in orientation. All classical science is contained already in the work of Eudoxus and Archimedes. Eudoxus, Plato's friend, and student of one of the last real Pythagoreans, to whom were attributed the theory of real numbers and the invention of the integral calculus, combined circular and straight movements carried out in the same sphere, but around different axes and with different velocities, in order to form a mechanical model that took into account and perfectly rendered all the facts known to his epoch concerning the stars. The idea of a single moving body accomplishing at the same time several different movements that were found in a specific trajectory is the foundation of kinetics, and alone lets one conceive of a combination of forces; we have only replaced circular movements by rectilinear ones, and introduced acceleration. There is the only difference between our conception of the motions of the stars and that of Eudoxus, for while Newton had often spoken of the force of attraction, gravitation is nothing other than a motion uniformly accelerated in the direction of the sun. Archimedes not only founded the science of statics but also mechanics by his purely mathematical theory of the balance, of the lever, and of the center of gravity; and his theory of the equilibrium of floating bodies, which is also purely mathematical, and which leads one to consider fluids as a system of superimposed levers where an axis of symmetry plays the role of a fulcrum, contains the germ of all physics. It is quite wrong that in teaching today that these marvelous conceptions are brought down to the level of empirical observations, and utterly denuded of interest. It is true that dynamics, founded on the consideration of uniformly accelerated motion, was a novelty to the sixteenth century; but, if thanks to the Bernoullis, d'Alembert, and Lagrange, we arrived at reducing all dynamics to a single formula, then this was done by bringing it back as much as possible to statics, by defining the cohesion of a system of bodies or of material points in motion as an equilibrium identical to that of the lever. Classical science is only an effort to conceive all things in nature as systems of levers, as Archimedes had done with water.

But if Greek science is the beginning of classical science, it is also, at the same time, something else. The concepts that it employs have all sorts of moving resonances and more than one meaning. Equilibrium, for example, was always at the center of Greek thought; it was in Egypt, too, for centuries and centuries, for there the balance was the symbol *par excellence* of equity, the first of the virtues in their eyes. Injustice appears, implicitly in the *Iliad*, and explicitly in Aeschylus, as a rupture of equilibrium that needs to be later compensated for by an opposite disequilibrium, and so on; a striking formula of Anaximander applies this conception to nature itself, making the entire course of natural phenomena appear as a succession of compensating, parallel disequilibria, a moving image of equilibrium as time is the moving image of eternity: "As birth causes things to arise from the indeterminate, destruction makes them return to it by necessity; for they suffer punishment and expiation by their mutual injustices according to the order of time." There are some lines in the *Gorgias*, the most beautiful ones perhaps, ringing the same note; Socrates there is reproaching the defender of injustice with ignoring the fact that concord and harmony determine the order of the world, and with forgetting geometry. The concept that appears in words like that is the same concept that, under the name of equilibrium, constitutes Greek physics. Archimedes only needed to find a rigorous definition for it; or, rather, two definitions, one geometrical, the other empirical. Motion, and more generally change, appeared to the Greeks as disequilibrium; thus, in the eyes of Archimedes, the sign of equilibrium was immobility. On the other hand, with respect to a system of bodies systematically situated around an axis, it is clear that a group of bodies situated on one side of the axis cannot exercise any action on a group situated on the other side, and such symmetry constitutes the geometrical definition of equilibrium. The postulate is that, for the systems under consideration, the two definitions coincide, and that in the case where there might be immobility without symmetry it is always possible nevertheless to discover a hidden symmetry, following a chain of rigorous mathematical demonstrations. All of that, though not explicitly enunciated by Archimedes, is clearly implied in his postulates, hypotheses, and theorems. On the other hand, the concept of equilibrium dominates all the forms of authentic art, and one can even say the same for proportion, that central notion of Greek geometry; with respect to the uniform and circular motions of Eudoxus, they make up a sort of dance; there is also a splendid page in the *Epinomis* on the dance of the stars, a dance that a Greek writer later compared to the dances done around a candidate for initiation into the mysteries of Eleusis. Just as classical science is the parent of technology, Greek science, although just as rigorous, if not more so, although no less aimed at seizing upon necessity no matter where it is, is essentially the parent of art, and above all, Greek art.

Classical science takes as its model for representing the world the relation between some desire and the conditions under which it can be accomplished, while suppressing the first term of this relation. The suppression cannot, however, be complete. This is why it bases itself on linear motion, for linear direction is the form of thought of every person who desires, for example, to be somewhere, to seize or hit something or someone; and it also bases itself on distance, a condition necessarily inherent in every desire of any being in time. In such a picture of the world, the good is everywhere absent, absent to the point that one will not even find a hint of its absence; for even the term of the relation that one is forced to suppress, the term that concerns the human, is entirely foreign to the good. Thus classical science is not beautiful; it neither touches the heart nor does it contain wisdom. One can understand why Keats hated Newton, and Goethe did not like him any better. It was quite different with the Greeks. Blessed men, in whom love, art, and science were only three barely different aspects of the same movement of the soul toward the good. We are miserable compared to them, and this while what made them great has been put into our hands.

According to an admirable image found in the Manichaeans, which certainly comes from an earlier time, the spirit is torn into pieces and dispersed throughout space, through extended matter. It is crucified on extension; after all, isn't the cross the symbol of extension, since it is made of two perpendicular directions that define it? The spirit is also crucified on time, scattered in pieces throughout time, and likewise rent. Space and time are a single and identical necessity sensed in two ways; there is no other necessity. The thinking being, in his most animal desire just as in his most elevated desire, is separated from himself by the distance that time puts between him as he is now and what he is tending towards, and, if he ever believes he has found himself, he loses himself immediately by disappearing into the past. What he is in a single instant is nothing, what he has been, what he will be do not now exist, and the extended world is made of all that escapes him, since what he is, is kept at a single point, as if on a chain or in a prison, powerless to be elsewhere until after having dispensed with time, and after having submitted to hardship and after having abandoned the point where he used to be. Pleasure nails him in place in his prison and to the present moment that he, however, loses, desire suspends him from the next moment, and makes the whole world disappear for one single object, and there is always pain in his sensing the tearing and dispersion of his thought through the juxtaposition of place and time. Yet, as a thinking being, he senses he has been made for something other than time and space; not being able to keep them from being present to his thought, he senses himself made at least to be their master, in order to inhabit eternity, to dominate and hold onto time, to possess all the extended universe all at once. The necessity of time and space oppose this. But the juxtaposition of things in extension that change from moment to moment, however, furnish us an image of this lost and forbidden sovereignty. If it were otherwise, one could not live; for it would be given to us only to think what we can sense. It is because of this image that the universe, although pitiless, merits our love, even at the moment when we are suffering from it, like a city or country does.

This image is provided to us in certain human works by the concepts of limit, order, harmony, proportion, or regular occurrences, all by which a human being is permitted to embrace by a single act of thought a juxtaposition of places equivalent to all places, a succession of instants equivalent to all instants, as if he were everywhere and always, and as if he were eternal. But in order that there be a true image of this looking down upon the world, and not an empty and cold lie, it is necessary that this act be difficult, that it seem to be on the verge of completion and yet never be achieved, and that the necessity of time and space that are opposed to it may be more painfully felt than in the most afflicted moments of life. A just blend of unity and that which opposes it, that is, then, the condition of the beautiful, and it is the secret of art, a mysterious secret for the artist and also the scientist. A series of sounds varies like the voice of someone who is a slave to emotions, submissive to change, submissive to obsession; however, the combinations of sounds are linked together by regular patterns where they seem at the same time identical to themselves and new, all in a way that the listener wanders through their forest even as he is chained to one place; silence surrounds this suite of sounds from one end to the other, marks it with a beginning and an end, and at the same time seems to prolong it indefinitely. A space may be enclosed by limits that one cannot modify and that seem to enclose a world apart but that also evoke unlimited distances outside itself, farther than the stars in every direction; one grasps it pretty much in a single glance at its structure, but it invites one to take a further step in which then develops in it an infinity of different aspects. A block of marble that one might believe to be fluid and flowing, that one might believe flexible to the pressure of the whole surrounding universe, has taken forever the form of an intact human body, in a pose of equilibrium where gravity cannot change it and where yet all motion seems equally possible. In a painting, a small surface encloses within well-marked limits an infinitely vast space of three dimensions, where things and beings are linked and separated by their reciprocal positions, apparently fixed in a single moment, and in such a way that it seems they are not being seen by anybody or from any point of view, as if they were surprised, unsullied by human regard and clothed in unawareness. A poem presents characters where each in his turn is the listener and then someone else, who all change as they are borne along by an unfeeling time marked by the meter of the verse, and yet by this meter the past remains and the future is here; the weight of the entire universe, under the form of affliction marks there all people without destroying any of them and changes the words without breaking the meter. All of these are images that touch and wound the soul at its center. A human body and face that inspire at the same time both desire, and, more strongly, the dread of approaching them, because of the fear of harming them, whose change we cannot imagine, and whose extreme fragility we intensely feel, which tears up our soul by the roots, and which makes us sense that we are nailed to them, is also that kind of image. And the universe foreign to the human also gives us these kinds of images.

The universe furnishes such images by the divine favor accorded to humans when applying number in a certain manner as an intermediary, as Plato put it, between the one and the indefinite, the unlimited, indeterminate, between the unity that humans can think and all that which opposes their attempts to think it. This intermediary is not the sort of number by which one counts, nor is it a number that comes from continually repeated addition, but rather is the number by which one can form relations or ratios; for a ratio between two numbers, something that is infinitely different than a fraction, is at the same time a ratio between an infinity of other numbers suitably chosen and grouped in pairs. Each ratio involves quantities that grow without limit but without ever ceasing to continue in a perfect relation, just as an angle, beginning at a single point encloses a space that extends indefinitely behind it, beyond the farthest stars. And the relation, in order to be thought, has to go beyond numbers into an angle, for whole numbers do not as easily lend themselves to ratio as they do to addition; they have no way of expressing, except in a few cases, the mean proportional. Not only must the Greeks of the archaic period have known how to do this, the Babylonians in 2000 BC did, too, for they were looking for solutions to second-degree equations, which is to say, for mean proportionals; the incommensurability of the diagonal of a square, belatedly revealed in Greece to the public at large, caused trouble and scandal only among the ignorant. The Greeks of the sixth century founded the study of real numbers, and henceforth the study of the world consisted in the search for numbers in this new sense, which is to say, for proportions. For the world has proportions to be found.

Thus instead of a relation between desire and the conditions of its fulfillment, Greek science had as its object the relation between order and the conditions of order. It is a question of an order that is sensible to the human, and consequently the human is not absent from this relation; yet, this order is better related to the universe than desire, effort, or the notion of a project is; Greek science is at least as non-anthropocentric as classical science, no matter what the boast of the nineteenth century was. The conditions that one seeks to define in the two relations are the same; it is the same necessity of space and time, obstacle and support, whether it is the work of an architect or anyone who creates order in no matter what kind of work. Moreover, to think the conditions of an order, this is to think a constructed order, it is to relate it to any order that is the result of work; on the other hand, all effective work supposes a certain order in the universe and certain proportions, without which there would be neither tool nor method; thus the two relations seem to run together. But the spirit of the two sciences is essentially different. The Greeks, above all where they thought they had discerned an order, constructed an image of it with perfectly defined elements and submitted it to necessity; if there was any divergence between this image and their observations, the difference signified the intervention in phenomena of factors other than the ones they had assumed. One cannot wish for anything more rigorous. But this perfect rigor was at the same time poetry.

Eudoxus's definition of proportion, which constitutes the theory of real numbers, is itself beautiful, enveloping the infinite variations that four magnitudes can undergo when multiplied two by two by all the possible whole numbers, without ever failing to obey the law that makes these products larger or smaller than one another. Still more beautiful was the first intuition of Thales when he saw in the sun the author of an infinity of proportions that are inscribed on the ground and that change with the shadows; from this first moment appeared the notion of variable proportion, which is to say, the notion of function; but for us the term "function" indicates the dependence of one term on another, whereas the Greeks simply found their joy making change an object of contemplation. If one adds a load to a boat, which lowers it a bit, we can see in that a force that produces an effect; in the eyes of Archimedes a line marked on the surface of a floating body was the image of a ratio between its density and that of the fluid. In the same way, a point marked on a balance in equilibrium puts the proportion between two unequal weights in terms of length. What more beautiful image than that of a boat kept up on the sea, like a pan in a balance, by a mass of seawater placed on the other side of an axis, and that changes without moving as the ship moves forward, like the shadow of a bird that flies? One loses this poetry, one also loses much of rigor, by speaking simply of a thing pushed higher. Although it may be easier to construct an elliptical trajectory with linear motions susceptible to acceleration than with uniform circular motions, we have lost the rigor and the poetry by talking of planets tending to the sun; it is more beautiful to say that the stars describe circles, and that their successive positions reflect the proportions between the radii, velocities, and angles defining the diverse circular movements inherent in them. The circle is the image of infinite motion and finite, changing and unchanging; it contains within itself a closed space and evokes all the concentric circles that extend as far as the universe; it is also, as Pythagoras recognized ecstatically, the locus of mean proportionals. Circular motion has a law, but is not directed in any way; it alone belongs to the stars, it alone can be applied to them without diminishing their power to evoke for us all that is eternal. The Greeks were right to think that one such example of fittingness sufficed to render a hypothesis legitimate, for nothing else could better legitimate it. Blind necessity, which holds us in by constraint and which appears to us in geometry, is, for us, something to conquer; for the Greeks it was something to love, for it is God himself who is the perpetual geometer. From Thales' flash of genius up to the moment when Roman arms wiped them out, in the regular recurrences of the stars, in sounds, in balances, in floating bodies, everywhere the Greeks applied themselves to reading these proportions as a way to love God.

Although it has taken different forms according to country and epoch, the knowledge of the world has for its object, its model, and its principle the relation between an aspiration of human thought and the effective conditions for its realization, a relation that we try to read through the appearances that the spectacle of the world presents, and upon this relation we construct an image of the universe. For example, magic is like classical science in the kind of human aspiration on which it focuses, namely, desire of some kind. What magic considers as the conditions needed to realize it, however, are rites and signs, which are, effectively, considerations for the success of human action, although they are variable by society. Greek science concerns itself with the same conditions as classical science, but it has an entirely different aspiration in mind, namely, the aspiration to contemplate an image of the good in sensible appearances. The aspiration that corresponds to what we call the traditional sciences seems to tend towards the powers that are analogous to those that a man can effectively acquire over himself and perhaps over others by a long effort of interior transformation; these conditions are mysterious. To the degree that there can be similar relations susceptible of being conceived by us, that is, the degree to which there are different forms of the knowledge of the world; and the value of each of these forms is the value of the relation that serves us as principle, no more, no less. Furthermore, some of these forms exclude each other; others exclude nothing. But what should we think of contemporary science? What relation serves it as principle and as its measure of value? It is difficult to answer this question, not that there is any obscurity in it, but because it is embarrassing. The philosophical significance of twentieth-century physics, its deepest thought and soul, is like the emperor's new clothes in Anderson's fairy tale; one would be taken for a fool and ignoramus for saying that they do not exist, so it is better to talk about them as beyond words. Nevertheless, the relation that is the principle of this science is simply the relation between algebraic formulations, void of meaning, and technology.[2]

Twentieth-century science is classical science after something has been taken away from it. Taken away, not added. We haven't contributed any notion to what classical science had, and we certainly have not filled in the absence that made it such a desert, namely, a relation to the good. We have subtracted from it the analogy between the laws of nature and the conditions of work, which is to say, its very principle; it is this that the quantum hypothesis has decapitated. The algebraic formulas to which the description of phenomena was reduced at the end of the nineteenth century still pointed at this analogy by the fact that one could make them correspond to a mechanical apparatus that translated the relations between distances and forces; that is not the case for a formula made up of a constant and a number; that kind of formula can express nothing bearing a relation to distance. If one suspends equal weights at different heights and one raises a pan that raises them in the degree that it contacts them, the variations of energy, which are a function of distance and force, resemble those of a surface bounded by two perpendicular straight lines, of which one is moving and the other a zigzag; put otherwise, they will be continuous. One can seek to imagine as many mechanical apparatuses as one likes involving discontinuity; in no case can a function of two variables of which one varies in a continuous manner be increased by the successive addition of a constant quantity. For energy is a function of space, and space is continuous; it is continuity itself; it is the world thought from the point of view of continuity; it is things in general insofar as their juxtaposition envelops the continuous. One can think of things as discontinuous, which is to say, as atoms—one cannot do otherwise without falling into contradictions— but even at the price of implicit contradictions one cannot think of space in this way. If certain Greeks, it is said, spoke of the number of points contained in a straight-line segment, it is only because they conceived number as the model of quantity, and because language lets you say anything. But we cannot think space as discontinuous any more than we can think of the continuous as discontinuous. We have nothing more certain to guide our affirmations than these impossibilities; space is continuous. Energy is a function of space; all variations of energy are analogous to what happens when weights fall or are lifted. Planck's formula, to wit, the constant 6.55×10^{-27}, or more briefly, the constant h, multiplied by a number, does not signify energy. But it does not signify a notion other than energy, either. It plays the same role in calculating as the old formula signifying energy, and is regarded as a limiting case of it for phenomena on the scale where the quantity 6.55×10^{-27}, related to the unit of energy measure, can be neglected. If the relation were inverted, if the quantum formula were a limit of the classical formula, meaning would be preserved; but that is not the case. For there does not exist in human thinking any notion of a relation to which the notion of the work of lifting a weight can be considered as a valid limit to a certain scale. Planck's formula, made up of a constant whose provenance one cannot imagine and a number corresponding to a probability, has no relation with any thought. How is one going to justify this? One can base its legitimacy on the number of calculations, of experiments based on these calculations, and of technical applications coming out of these experiments, which have succeeded thanks to this formula. Planck himself alleged nothing more. But once this is admitted, physics becomes a grab bag of signs and numbers combined in some formulas that are controlled by their applications. After this, what importance can the speculations of Einstein on space and time have? The letters and the formulas by which it translates the words "space" and "time" have no more relation with space and time that the letters hv have to energy. Pure algebra has become the language of physics, a language that has this feature in particular: it expresses nothing. This particularity makes it difficult to translate.

This upending of physics is the result of two changes: the introduction of the discontinuous and the perfecting of measuring instruments that changed the scale of our observations. Chemistry was born the day when a balance made the simple and fixed numeric relations between distinct substances that are combined appear; in that measurement it was already implied that the discontinuous and number would return to the forefront of the science of nature. On the other hand, the new apparatuses gave us access to the observation of phenomena that were on a scale too small for us to sense, such as Brownian motion. Discontinuity, number, smallness, that is enough to give rise to the atom, and the atom has reappeared in our midst with its inseparable train of retainers, that is to say, chance and probability. The appearance of chance in science has been a scandal; we want to know where it came from, yet only have to reflect that the atom brought it; one only has to remember that already in the ancient world chance went along with atoms, and one has never dared to think that it could be otherwise.

We are often mistaken about chance. Chance is not the contrary of necessity; it is not incompatible with necessity. On the contrary, it never appears except at the same time as necessity. If one takes a certain number of distinct causes producing effects according to a rigorous necessity, if a set with a certain structure appeared in the effects, but if one cannot group their causes in a set with the same structure, then there is chance. A die, because of its form, can only land in six ways, but there are an unlimited number of ways of throwing it. If I throw a die a thousand times, the results can be put into six classes that have numeric relations between them; the throws cannot be so organized. Moreover, I cannot imagine the least break in the tissue of mechanical necessities that determine each movement of the die. If I throw the die once, I do not know what the result will be, not because of an indetermination in the phenomenon, but because it is a problem where in part I do not know the givens. It is not this ignorance that gives me the sense of chance, but uniquely the image, which accompanies my movement, of an indefinite number of other possible movements whose effects also fall into six classes. It is the same thing if I were to consider the set of possible colored positions on a board game that the pointer of a turning disk could land on and the impulses that could be given to it to get it to turn. In such games, the set of causes has the power of the continuous, which is to say, that the causes are like the points of a line; the set of effects are defined by a small number of distinct possibilities. In antiquity, the image of atoms immediately brought to mind games of chance, and it was not a mere fancy, despite the differences. If I conceive under the name of the universe a set of moving atoms, each motion being strictly determined, and if I ask myself how the phenomena unfold on a macrocosmic level, which to the eyes of the observers of the atoms remains invisible, I absolutely could not conceive any reason for constancy from their current unfolding, any regularity, any coordination, or even that one might be able to have an experience a second time. It is clear that if one cannot experience something the same way twice, there is no physics. Conceiving atoms quickly makes the success of physics on the human scale look like an accident.

The link between two physics, the physics of atoms and the physics of the phenomena that we perceive, can only be established by probability. Probability is inseparable from chance, and by it, chance is an experimentally controllable notion. When, in games of chance, I consider the continuous set of causes and the small number of categories into which their effects can be distributed, I affirm that, though each effect proceeds rigorously from a cause, there is absolutely nothing in the set of causes that corresponds to these categories; that is what it means to say that there is chance. Hence these categories all have an identical relation to the set of causes that, at the same time, is indifferent to them. That is what it means to say that they are all equally probable. The notion of probability always implies a distribution into equal probabilities. If I consider for a moment a die on which five faces bear the number "one" and the remaining one the number "two," there are always six equal probabilities, but five of them coincide; that is the only way that one can conceive unequal probabilities. With respect to the relation of probability to experiment, it is analogous to the relation of necessity to experiment; the experiment presents an image of necessity when, by varying a cause, one gets effects that vary as a function; it presents an image of probability when the distribution of effects into categories gets closer and closer to the proportions indicated by calculation as the effects accumulate. If the experiment resists such an image, one proceeds as when it refuses an image of necessity; you suppose that you have forgotten certain factors in your calculations.

The task of classical physics when brought to bear upon atoms was difficult. It had to conceive of very small indivisible particles, whose movements were subject to classical mechanics; these movements had to be such that they could be united by the necessities belonging to phenomena observable only at the microscopic level and, by rigorously reconstructed probabilities, to the phenomena observable at the human level, whose regular variations up until then had been the sole object of physics. Classical physics regarded a stone that had been lifted as a single point describing a vertical, rectilineal trajectory; it regarded, in essence, the whole stone as a single atom, and that is how it calculated energy. If in its place one imagines the complicated combinations of movements that describe the particles of the stone and of the air, it is necessary, thanks to the notions of chance, probabilities, averages, and approximations to recover the formula previously calculated. It is either necessary to establish such a link between the two physics or completely renounce one of them. That at least seems evidently what ought to be done; but things turned out differently. One can only establish this link by supposing that the atoms bow to different necessities than those of classical physics.

As all of science was reduced to the study of energy, a very strange transformation took place in this study, completely made over by the intermediary of new hypotheses for the molecular scale. Planck explains how it happened. He was looking for a way to express a relation between energy and temperature. To this end, he considered a case where the system of exchanges of energy between bodies depends solely on temperature and not on the nature of the bodies; such was, according to Kirchhoff, the case with blackbody radiation, which is to say, it is the case with an enclosed space where the temperature was uniform. Apparently, this is why it sufficed to reconstruct a particular case of blackbody radiation in mathematical terms, choosing a reconstruction that made use of a function that would link energy to temperature. With this in mind, Planck chose Hertzian oscillators. The first attempt failed. But then, no longer looking for the relation between energy and temperature, but between energy and entropy, he found that the second derivative of entropy with respect to energy is proportional to the energy. But, if this relation is verified by experiment in the case of short wavelengths, it soon appeared that for large ones this second derivative was proportional to the square of the energy. Planck easily found a formula covering the two relations; but this did not satisfy him. He wanted to reconstruct it. With this in view, he adopted Boltzmann's point of view, namely, that entropy, related to atoms, is the measurement of a probability, and he rediscovered for this probability the same formula that he had sought to find, but on the condition of taking into account two constants, of which one had a relation to the mass of the atom, and of which the other, 6.55×10^{-27}, was nothing other than this constant h that has become so celebrated by posterity, and that corresponded to an energy multiplied by a time. Such a constant has no sense in relation to classical mechanics, but "it is only thanks to it that we can understand the domains or indispensable intervals for the calculation of probabilities"; for, "the calculation of the probability of a physical state rests on the enumeration of the finite number of equally probable particular cases by which the state under consideration is realized."

It clearly appears in these lines of Planck that what is being introduced here is discontinuity, not because of any experiment—although experimental measures had necessarily played a role in the determination of the number 6.55×10^{-27}—but entirely because of the usage of the notion of probability. There is a natural transition between the notion of entropy and that of probability, by the consideration that, if a system, isolated from external disturbance, can pass from state A to state B, but cannot go the other way, by no matter what chain of intermediaries, then state B is more probable than state A in relation to the system. At the same time that these conceptions were to be elaborated, chance as linked to the atom also appeared. The observation of Brownian motion showed that a fluid that is homogeneous and in a state that is on a scale our eyes can detect, is neither homogeneous nor at rest on a microscopic scale; this was hardly surprising. Now, a fluid in equilibrium is perfectly defined, on the human scale, by the conditions of equilibrium, while we have no means, in fact, of defining the state of equilibrium of this same fluid on the molecular scale. In a general way, a system defined by our scale is not at the molecular level; one can only suppose the atomic system would appear to us at our scale as the one we have. But if one establishes for it this sort of correspondence, more than one combination of atoms will correspond to a well-defined state on our scale; what follows is that if one introduces necessity among the atoms, each of these possible combinations will be liable to bring about, at a later moment, a different state of the system. Thus, once one introduces necessity into the atomic system, then the relation between two states of the system defined on our scale will not constitute a necessity but a probability. This is not because of any hole in causality, but only because of an inevitable effect of the oscillation of thought as it moves back and forth between the two scales, and by a process analogous to that of a game of dice. A natural movement of thought leads us to bring together the two probabilities simultaneously arising in our minds, the one linked to entropy and the other linked to atoms, and to look at them as one and the same probability. This assimilation was Boltzmann's work.

One starts with the idea that with atoms there are only necessities, which are only mechanical necessities, and no differences in probability, and so it follows that all combinations of atoms are equally probable. One considers a system and a state of this system defined on our scale, and the number of combinations of atoms that can correspond to it; the probability of this state is a function of this quantity, and one assumes that entropy is a measure of this probability. But as the calculation of probabilities is a numeric calculation, one has to assume—and here is where the break with classical science occurs—that these atomic combinations are, as it is said, discrete, and that their quantity is a number. Thus, entropy is the function of a number, although we defined it in the beginning, when it was invented, as a function of energy that increases when it takes, at least partially, the form of heat. The contradiction is the same as if one were to say, for example, that a quantity that is defined as a function of the distance run by a runner is also the same quantity as the number of steps he has taken. It is this contradiction that appears in the idea of quanta of atoms of energy, and it is this that has taken from science, beginning in 1900, the meaning that it had over the course of the previous four centuries, without giving it anything to replace it. The rupture between the science of the twentieth century on the one hand, and classical science and common sense on the other, was total before Einstein's paradoxes; an infinite and measurable speed, time that is a fourth dimension of space, are not more difficult things to conceive than an atom of energy; all that is equally impossible to conceive, no matter how easy it is to formulate whether in the language of algebra or in everyday language.

Did science have to take this direction—if one can even speak of "direction" when it has stopped being directed? It does not seem at all evident. Since the cause of the break of continuity was the numeric calculation of probabilities, it is difficult to understand, at first sight, why no one had chosen to work on the calculation of probabilities rather than standing physics on end. One can conceive of probabilities that are neither whole numbers nor fractions. If one supposes, for example, that one might turn a disc with a pointer, and that the pointer spun around an immobile circumference on which there is a red section, then the probability of the pointer stopping on the red will be measured by the relation of the arc to the circumference, a relation that cannot be a fraction, that is, a rational number; one can easily conceive a calculation of probabilities of which the base is not a whole or rational number, but a real number. In order to apply such a calculation to Boltzmann's theory, it would be necessary to conceive a continuous set of combinations of atoms corresponding to a system defined at the human scale, and to find the means of making a magnitude analogous to distance correspond to such a set, compared to other sets of the same type. At first sight, that seems impossible. But has anyone tried to spell out such a theory and then failed? In any case, what is the cause of the failure? Or has anyone even dared to try, despite the extreme simplicity of such an idea? It is certain in any case that here is the crucial point in any critical examination of quantum theory; it is certain that Planck succeeded in writing a book, recently translated, on the relations of contemporary science and philosophy, without making any sort of allusion to it.

Although the good was absent from classical science, as long as the intellectual work in science was only a sharpened form of the elaboration of the notions of common sense, there was at least some link between scientific thought and the rest of human thought, and thereby it included the thought of the good. But this same link, already so indirect, was broken after 1900. Self-styled philosophers, weary of reason, without doubt because reason was so demanding, gloried in the idea of a lack of accord between science and reason; of course, they blamed reason for being wrong. What gave them particular joy was thinking that a simple change of scale brings a radical transformation of the laws of nature, whereas reason demanded that a change of scale change the magnitudes, and not the ratios between magnitudes; or again, they were happy to think that necessities that had long been regarded as evident had become approximations, when better instruments let them, thanks to atoms, penetrate further into the structure of phenomena. Their joy was not only impious, being directed against reason, it witnessed to a singularly opaque incomprehension. The study of atoms corresponds in science, not only to a change in scale, but also to a change in everything else. If one were to imagine a little man, like us, but of the size of an atomic particle, living among atoms, this little man, by hypothesis, would sense heat, light, sounds at the same time that he perceived and accomplished motion. Yet in the atomic world as conceived by physicists, there is only motion. In going from our world to that of atoms we transform, among other things, heat and motion; for our sensibility there is a difference not in size but in the very nature of heat and motion. There is also a difference in the nature of heat and motion in relation to the conditions of our work. Not only can we never hope, when we make an effort, to obtain a result from any procedure that is greater than belongs to our effort—the principle of the conservation of energy forbids this hope—but we cannot hope to get the full result that belongs to our effort. We lose some of what we put out whenever we make an effort in the world, and this loss, origin of the notion of entropy, is measured by heat; there is for us a difference between this lost energy and the used energy as, for example, the difference, for a worker, between his tool getting hot and the production of pieces in the factory. This is why there is only motion, but not heat, in the purely theoretical world of atoms, so in relation to this world by itself, entropy has no sense; and this is why, to give it a sense in relation to this world and to ours considered together, it is necessary to interject this probability that has destroyed classical physics. The cause of it is not in the change of dimensions, but the attempt to define entropy, a notion essentially foreign to motion, by motion alone.

Moreover, a change of scale ought necessarily to produce an upheaval in physics by reason of the role played by the negligible. Whenever general considerations of physics are brought up, one passes over
this notion quickly as by a sort of repression or out of a sense of shame.
Physicists not only neglect what is negligible, as by definition they
ought to do, but they are also inclined to neglect the concept of the
negligible, which is quite precisely the essence of physics, all the while
they are making use of it. The negligible is nothing other than what is
necessary to neglect in order to construct physics; it is not what is of
little importance, for what is neglected is always an infinite error. What
is neglected is as big as the world, exactly as big, for a physicist neglects
all the differences between a thing that is before his eyes, and a perfectly
closed system, perfectly defined as he conceives it in his mind and represents it on paper by images and signs; and this difference is the world
itself, the world that is pressed around each bit of matter, that infiltrates
it from inside, that puts an infinite variety of things between two points
no matter how close they are; the world is what absolutely keeps there
from being any closed system. One neglects the world because it is necessary to do so, and not being able to apply mathematics to things at a
lesser cost, one applies mathematics at the cost of an infinite error.

Mathematics itself even implies an infinite error insofar as it needs
objects and images. If I see two stars, I imagine a line between the two
of them, the purest possible line, since it is not drawn; but it is hardly
the case that the stars are points, since they are bigger than the earth
itself. If I draw a chalk line on a blackboard, I get, since here there can
be no question of the scale of magnitudes, something that differs as
much from a straight line as a whole ocean, something infinitely different than a straight line. And, yet, it is something that is not without
a relation to a straight line. The relation consists in this: that the chalk
on the blackboard lets me imagine the straight line; it is only in this
sense that the figures are images of geometric notions, not that they
resemble them, but that they let us imagine them. It is that alone that
allows one to say that a chalk line is more or less a straight line. Now, in
a sense, an observation or an experiment is exactly for a physicist what
a figure is for a geometer. Plato, who knew that the straight line of
geometry is not the one that is drawn, also knew that the stars that describe uniform and circular motion are not the ones we see at night; and

Archimedes, who had read Plato, certainly knew, without needing to observe Brownian motion, that there is no homogeneous fluid or fluid at perfect rest in nature; he knew also that the beam of a balance is matter and not a geometrical line. In our time, entropy has been calculated from a relation between energy, volume, and temperature in perfect gases, which are called "perfect gases" because they do not actually exist.

A geometer whenever he examines a problem conceives a system perfectly defined by certain elements — position, distances, angles — that he himself has given to it; he draws a figure to help him imagine these elements; if it leads him at the same time to imagine something else than what he has given to it, either he abstracts it or he changes the figure; but in any case, he does not give himself the license to imagine something other than what he has put into it and what is expressible in a small number of phrases. In the same way, the physicist, when he studies a phenomenon, conceives a perfectly defined system, perfectly closed, where he allows entry only to what he himself puts into it and what is expressible in a few phrases. Often he represents his system the way a mathematician does, by figures or by formulas; but he represents it also by objects, and that is what doing an experiment is. His system contains, or does not contain, a factor of change; in the first case, the physicist mentally leads the system he has defined from an initial state to a final one by the intermediary of necessity; and he will then look for an experimental apparatus in which the initial state above all imitates the initial state of the closed system, as a triangle drawn in chalk imitates a theoretical triangle, and whose transformation then has the same relation with it as the one in the closed system. If it is a question of a state of equilibrium, on the contrary, then the experimental apparatus should stay immobile. Naturally, sometimes it works, and sometimes it does not.

If it does not work, the physicist can modify his experimental apparatus in order to better mirror the theoretical system, just as a geometer erases a figure and then draws it more carefully; after which, one more time, it will work or it will not. He can also decide that his system is impossible to mirror with objects, and he can use another slightly different one through which he hopes to succeed at the same job; of course, as he does so, he will take into account his previous failure. But the order is always the same; the experimental apparatus is always a mirroring of a purely theoretical system, and that is the case even when the system has been reworked after an experimental failure. He cannot do it any other way; one cannot think of necessity differently. For necessity is essentially conditional, and it appears to the human mind only as the set of a small number of distinct and perfectly defined conditions; this is the only way that a thinker can present this idea to himself, in his mind, as a hypothesis, and via a certain number of perfectly definite conditions; for the conditions that the world in fact imposes on his action are unlimited, without number, inexpressible, and that is why he always has to expect to be surprised. Moreover, in giving himself a perfectly closed system, that is, one where he does not let anything else into it, one of perfectly determined conditions of a finite number, and then looking for whatever necessities and impossibilities that might appear, he is doing mathematics. The mathematical method, no matter what it is applied to, is nothing else; and it follows in full measure that where the notion of necessity plays a role in physics, physics is essentially the application of mathematics to nature at the price of an infinite error.

But when one has understood that the lines drawn by the geometer and that the things that are the objects of observation or of experiment by the physicist are mirrors or imitations of mathematical concepts, one has still understood only a little. For one yet is unaware of that in which this relation consists, what we can call, for lack of a better name, imitation. I press the chalk twice on the blackboard; twice I get something other than a straight line, other and infinitely different; however, it appears to me that the first one was a little closer to straightness, and the second one was more of a curved line. What is the difference between these two deposits of chalk? The geometer can leave that alone as a side issue, since what interests him is only the straight line; the physicist cannot, for he is not interested in pure closed systems built in his mind by the help of signs and figures, but in the relation of things to these systems. This relation is impenetrably obscure. If one examines the simplest example, the straight line, one finds that what brings the human mind to think about the straight line is directed movement, which is to say, the project of movement; the things he sees that lead him to think of a straight line are, first, that of a point, that is, a place to which he intends to go, or that of two points, if he is thinking about a path leading from one to the other, or that of a movement's mark accomplished while thinking of a straight line, the chalk mark on a blackboard, of a pencil on paper, of a stick in the sand, or any other such mark. It is because one has pressed the chalk on the blackboard while thinking about a straight line when he presses that he is led by what he sees there to think about a straight line. This kinship between motion and what we see, the foundation of perception, is a mystery; it only takes contemplating certain drawings of Rembrandt or Leonardo, for example, to sense how moving this mystery is.

This isn't the only mystery linked to the straight line; there are others, all impenetrable, and on which the only clarity one can bring is enunciating them and distinguishing them. We are aware each time that we think of them that the pure straight line, the pure angle, the pure triangle, are works of the attention that make the effort of detaching these things from sensible appearances and actions; but the necessities, the impossibilities that are attached to them, which are imposed on our minds, where do they come from? For example, the impossibility of counting the points on a straight line or the impossibility of joining two points by more than one straight line? We can refuse to admit certain of these, as has been done in the case of the latter, and as one cannot dare to do in the case of the former, but even for the most profound mathematician, non-Euclidean geometries are not on the same plane as Euclidean geometry; we believe in the Euclidean despite ourselves but cannot entirely believe in the others, and we must, in order to explicate them, imagine curved lines whenever we say "straight line." Secondly, the effort of attention necessary to detach oneself from things in order to think a point, a line, a pure angle, can only be accomplished by leaning on things, and the deposited chalk, the sand imprinted by human movements, or certain objects, constitute indispensable aids. Furthermore, one cannot use just any object to imagine the concept, but there are for our imagination certain links between a specific thing and the specific concepts that we form when we detach ourselves from things. Finally, whenever we see a place where we want to go, we head off there by thinking of a direction, which is a straight line; and while we may be aware of accomplishing at the same time movements that are infinitely different from the trajectory of a straight line, we most often end up at the place we wanted to go. A branch of a tree, blown by the wind, though it may bend a bit, leads me to think of a straight line in relation to the angle. If I break it, slip it under a stone and push on the other end in order to lift the stone up, I am still thinking about the straight line in relation to the angle; and although there is nothing in common between the branch of the tree and a straight line, and I know it, I often am successful. The purity of mathematical notions, the necessities and impossibilities that are attached to them, the indispensable images of these concepts furnished by things that don't resemble them, the success of the actions undertaken by confounding, by a voluntary error, things with the concepts of which they are the images, these are so many distinct and irreducible mysteries, and if one works out a solution for one of them, one does not lessen, but, on the contrary, expands the impenetrable mystery of the others. For example, by admitting that geometrical relations are really the laws of the universe, one renders even more astonishing the success of actions ruled by a deliberately and infinitely erroneous application of these same relations; if one admits that they are simple summaries drawn from a bunch of successful relations, one fails to take account of either the necessity that is attached to them and that does not show up in these summaries, or one is taking account of the purity that is essential to them and that makes them foreign to the world; and so on. In thinking about geometry, we always think that the straight line is something pure, a work of the mind, foreign to appearances, foreign to the world; that there are necessities attached to it; that these necessities are really the very laws of the universe; that certain things in the world, which lead us to imagine the straight line, and without which we could not think it, are infinitely other than that straight line; that in acting as if they were straight lines that our action will succeed. There is more than one contradiction. It is a strange thing, these contradictions that are impossible to eliminate are what give geometry its value. They reflect the contradictions of the human condition.

A physicist who sets up a support for a balance and hangs two weights, equal or unequal, from its ends is thinking about a straight line turning around a fixed point, all the while knowing that there is neither a fixed point nor a straight line in front of him; a straight line is not something that a blow can bend or break or that fire can burn. The physicist does with this beam what the geometer does with his chalk marks; he does even more. The chalk follows the hand of the geometer, and the chalk mark remains immobile on the blackboard until someone takes an eraser to it; the geometer makes some simple diagrams on a surface, which are unchanged for the course of his meditations, except for his touching them up. The physicist manipulates objects in three-dimensional space, and after having set them up, he leaves them alone and exposed to change. Thus left alone, they sometimes continue to evoke in the imagination of the physicist the same mathematical concepts that they evoked when he set them up; the experiment then has succeeded. This way of defining a successful experiment seems strange, and yet it is not possible to define the relation by which objects are the images of mathematical concepts without the intermediary of the human imagination. If, as has often been claimed, what the physicist neglects in the experiment were an error that one can render as small as one would like, the voluntary omission of the negligible would constitute a passage to the limit in the sense of integral calculus, and the concept of the negligible would have a mathematical significance. But that is not the way it is; it is never that way, even in the best cases. In fact, it is not true that one can, by careful efforts, produce a surface as smooth as one would like; in a given age, in a given stage of technology, we can produce a given surface, more or less polished to a given degree, and this is the best one is going to get at this point, and one cannot go beyond it; it is always permitted to suppose that perhaps later on better technical procedures will produce more polished surfaces, but we do not know if that will happen or not. But if one considers a balance beam, it is quite clear that any technical progress will never produce anything that resembles a straight line turning around a fixed point. Strange as this seems, a physicist, looking at a balance beam knowing that it is not straight, but led by what he is looking at to imagine a straight line, chose to give more due to his imagination than to his reason. Archimedes did it this way, neglecting the infinite difference that separates a beam on a balance from a straight line, and so he invented physics. We still do it this way today. But, to speak truly, it had been done that way for unnumbered centuries before Archimedes; exactly as many as the balance has been in use.

Humans have always been tempted to give themselves a closed, limited universe that is rigorously defined; they have succeeded perfectly in certain games where all the possibilities are enumerable and even finite, such as games of dice, cards, and chess. The black and white squares of the chessboard, the game pieces, the possible movements of each, given the rules, are finite, and a game of chess being something that has to end sooner or later, then all possible games of chess are in fact a finite number, however complicated calculating them might be. It is the same, for example, for all possible games of the French card game of belote played with thirty-two cards. That the calculation is complicated is essential to the game's being interesting; no one would play it if he could, in fact, keep in mind all the possible games; but no matter that it exceeds the capacity of the human mind, as if it were infinite, it is finite all the same, and that, too, is essential to the game. The player gives himself a finite universe bounded by a rule that he imposes on his actions, and that each time he goes to play gives him a choice from only a small number of possibilities; but it is also bounded by solid objects, which he is led to imagine as immutable, although nothing is immutable in this world, and that he then takes by choice to treat as absolutely immutable. If he is stumped at certain times by the sight of a broken pawn, of a torn card, he says it is an accident, and he fixes it by replacing it with a new object, substituted for the broken and changed one, and treated as if nothing had happened. Every intervention into the universe of the closed system of the game is called an accident, and the accidents are neglected by the player. The game is thus the model of physics. There are other games where the possibilities are not of a finite number; however, they do form a well-defined set; in these games, real numbers play the role that rational numbers played in the first group of games. These are games such as ball games where more or less round objects are taken as spheres, and played on surfaces regarded as planes, such as bowling, billiards, or boules. In these games, too, there is a closed system determined by solid objects whose form is regarded as immutable, where fixed rules are imposed on movements limiting their possibilities, although the set of possibilities gives the effect of the continuous, and accidents are ignored.

Accidents can be ignored in games precisely because they are games. They are more difficult to ignore in work, where hunger, cold, sleep, and need flog us without end, where results are what matter, where an accident can render all our efforts pointless, or can cause affliction or death. Nevertheless, the concept of accident also has a sense for the worker, too; it is essential to work, and accidents are always what, in a sense, we neglect, at least in our project, and thus we can conjecture that work has borrowed this concept from play. Work in this case proceeds from play, imitates play, an imitation that perhaps one can find a vestige of in the morals of certain so-called primitives, more clearly than in ourselves. For each human being, in any case, play precedes work. Work is analogous to games where the possibilities form a continuous set; as in games, solid objects, whose form is considered immutable, whose deformation of any kind is considered an accident, serve as an instrument to classify and define possibilities, and as in games certain rules determine the movements. The worker, too, like the player, in however the slightest degree—for he cannot get rid of at any instant the results of actions he has taken and start over again—lives in a closed, limited, and defined world, thanks to the tools and to the rules for action that he has been given. I use a shovel by taking it in my hand, putting my foot on the blade, while communicating through my body, in relation to the shovel, defined attitudes; I work with it while thinking of the straight line in its relation with the angle; and all the variety of matter that the shovel meets is ordered in a series of continuous magnitudes, according to the greater or lesser degree of resistance that each movement encounters. What is more uncertain and varied than the sea and the wind? But a boat is a fixed solid, on which one chooses only to communicate, while working the sail and the helm, changes that form a continuous series, but perfectly defined; it cannot admit any change except one that comes from outside the series, unless as the effect of an accident; the sailor, in sailing the ship, while experiencing the push of the wind on the sails, and the water on the helm, thinks of orientations, rectilinear movements, the straight line in relation to the angle; and the infinitely varied states of the sea and air are ordered into a series defined by the relation of the state of the sail and helm, to the orientation and the speed of the boat that corresponds to each. Tools are instruments to order sensible appearances, to combine them in defined systems, and in working them, the worker is always thinking of the straight line, the angle, the circle, the plane; these thoughts direct his action, and it is at the price of an infinite error that he neglects them.

Humans need to give themselves defined systems by fixing for themselves rules for motion, and making solid objects of well-defined form, instruments for play or work, or, like the balance, of measurement. They do not find such defined systems ready-made in nature around them, or, rather, they find only one. This is the one that constitutes the stars. The stars are separate, distinct objects; the appearance of many of them is immutable if it isn't altered by the accident of the clouds. The number of them that one can see with the naked eye or certain instruments is finite, however huge that number may be; the appearances of the night sky corresponding to the different phases of the moon, to the various relative positions of the sun, the moon, the planets, the stars, are ordered in a perfectly definite series. The appearances of the night sky form a system so rigorously defined, so well closed, so well defended against accidents, except for a few, such as shooting stars and comets, that certain games alone can furnish human thought a set of combinations quite so manageable; but even there, the choice of the player at each move gives to games an arbitrary element that is not found among the stars, and the waiting of the player who is thinking about his next move, an uncertain and variable element in any match, keeps there from being in any game the same invariable rhythm that reigns in heaven. The stars, those marvelous, brilliant objects, inaccessible at least as far as the horizon, that we can never either change or touch, which touch only our eyes, are what are farthest from and closest to the human being; they alone in the universe respond to the first need of the human soul; they are like a toy given to us by God. Divination, which is sometimes done by cards, is also sometimes done using the stars; there is a natural relation between a system defined by possibilities and divination. There is also a natural relation between such systems and science. The stars, games such as boules, billiards, dice, the common instruments of measure such as the balance, tools and simple machines, all of these things have always been, par excellence, the objects of meditation for scientists. But the more the stars lend themselves to science, the more they are mysterious, for this harmony is a gift, a mystery, a matter of grace. The Greeks, who attributed uniform and circular movements to them, explained these movements by the perfection of the stars and their divine character. Classical astronomy never gave a more positive explanation, for the attraction at a distance that Newton talked about does not respond to what human thought demands in its search for causes. How does one conceive the space that separates two stars, a locus that undoubtedly, as all spaces are, is full of infinitely varied events, yet that never determines any change in the relation of the things it unites? And, despite the perfection of our telescopes and the sophisticated research of spectroscopy, we still do not know any more about it today; we cannot know more about it; the fittingness of the stars with the needs of the human imagination is an irreducible mystery. Games and tools at first seem less mysterious, since they are man-made. But that we can make such objects, and work with them on the supposition that they are, barring accidents, immutable, working with them all the while thinking about spheres, circles, planes, points, or right angles, working with them so effectively, that is a matter of grace that is just as extraordinary as the existence of the stars. It is one and the same grace, and, strange as it may be, the object of scientific study is nothing other than this grace.

In thinking mathematically, we bracket the world, and at the end of this effort of renunciation the world is then given to us as a value added—at the price of infinite error, of course, but really given. By this renunciation of things, by this contact with reality that accompanies that renunciation like a gratuitous recompense for the effort, geometry is an image of virtue. To pursue the good we turn ourselves away from things and then receive the world as our reward; as the straight line traced by a piece of chalk is what one traces with chalk while thinking of the straight line, so, too, the act of virtue is what one accomplishes while loving God, and as a drawn straight line, it encloses an infinite error. The grace that permits miserable mortals to think, to imagine, to effectively apply geometry, and to think, at the same time, that God is a perpetual geometer, and the grace that links the stars, dances, eyes, and our labors is marvelous, but it is not more marvelous than the existence of the human being itself, for such is the condition of those things. The human being, such as he is, delivered over to appearances, to sorrows, to desires, and yet destined for something else, is infinitely different from God and still obliged to be perfect as his heavenly Father is, he would not exist without such grace. The mystery of this grace is inseparable from the mystery of the human imagination, from the mystery of the relation that unites in us thoughts and movements, and it is inseparable from the consideration of the human body. The science of nature, which is one of the effects of this grace, only studies, other than in the case of the stars, objects made by human labor, and made according to mathematical notions. In the physicist's laboratory, in a museum of physics such as the *Palais de la Découverte*, everything is artificial; there are only apparatuses; and in the smallest parts of an apparatus how much labor, pain, time, ingenuity, and care have been expended by humans! This is not nature that is being studied here. How astonishing is the role that the scale of the human body plays in science, for it, at first sight, is one that is greater than any scale of magnitudes should play.

Physics explores the domain where it is permitted to the human being to succeed by applying mathematics at the price of an infinite error. The nineteenth century, the century that believed in unlimited progress, that believed people would get richer and richer, that a constant technological revolution would permit them to play more and more while working less and less, that education would render them more and more reasonable, that democracy would penetrate more and more into the public morals of every country, that century also believed that this domain was simply the whole universe. This century, exclusively attached to precious, but not ultimate, goods, believed that it had found the infinite in them; it was less afflicted than our century, but it was stifling; affliction is worth more. Despite the pride that we have inherited from the nineteenth century, and that, despite our misery, we have not taken the trouble to shake off, it is often better, even today, to inquire of an old peasant rather than a meteorologic institute if one is curious about the next day's weather. Clouds, rain, storms, wind are still today in large part beyond the domain where we can substitute things, with any success, for systems defined by us; and who knows if that will not be forever? In the domains, where, in the middle of the nineteenth century, such substitutions were possible, scientists had come to establish a certain unity, a certain coherence. That was not done without many efforts and groping about. Human thought does not have perfect freedom, but it does have a certain freedom in its choice of rigorously defined systems, where it can substitute for things or for such and such a phenomenon, and can thus choose in view of the greatest possible coherence what it will decide to overlook. The history of the gropings of science is in great part, perhaps entirely, the history of the different and successive applications of the concept of the negligible.[3]

For all time, undoubtedly, beginning in play and proven by work, humans have formed the concept of inert matter, which budges only when one pushes it. The concept of immobility is a definite notion. On the other hand, the concept of motion is not definite, because at the same time that a change is taking place, time intervenes in it. In every epoch perhaps, and in any case, that of the Greeks, uniform motion has appeared as the form of motion that is defined and that defines all other motion, just as the straight line is defined and defines all other lines; and the Greeks attributed uniform motion to the stars, because they were perfect and free of all accidents. They didn't have any other reason; one cannot have any other; for how can one measure motion without measuring time, and how does one measure time? The hypothesis of uniform motion gives an account of the regularity in celestial appearances, but one could also give an account of the regularity by attributing it to the celestial sphere, or to the sun, or to the moon, or the varied movements of the planets, if one makes them vary harmoniously. We do it differently today, barring the notion of the celestial sphere, since we attribute to the stars acceleration; but not to the motion of the rotation of the earth. But why not to this motion, too, unless because, respecting the fixed stars that still divide day from night, we still hold the same piety that animated the Greeks? This is a uniform motion, which has always signified, and that still signifies today, a fixed relation to the fixed stars. It cannot be otherwise. The things around us hardly move except when pushed; animals, which are the exception, seem to us to move either capriciously or by needs similar to ours; the wind, which in its irregular movement, often sudden and violent, appears always pushing and never pushed; to which the *Iliad* compares ceaselessly the impetus to victory, only known to us by the things that it pushes. The stars do not push, nor are pushed, are not stopped, bump into nothing; to our eyes they appear to proceed without impulsion or resistance; in seeing them inclined around the pole, how does one not help but to think on seeing their movement that this is uniform motion? But the Greek conception of circular and uniform motion as perfect motion, removed from exterior actions, does not absolutely permit us to define the movements that are produced on earth and around us.

In order to define these motions, Galileo had the daring to invent a point of departure by neglecting a universal fact of experience, namely, that excepting the stars, everything in motion ends at some moment by coming to a stop. We are so used to believing today that the principle of inertia is self-evident that we are sometimes naively surprised that antiquity and the Middle Ages did not recognize it; but, far from being a matter of evidence, this is a paradox. The movements of the stars, which are too slow to appear to us as motion, and that we have not, for this reason, any difficulty in thinking of as circular, are the only things that never stop; movements accomplished by us, brought about by us, or that we see being produced around us, and that are always accompanied in our thought by the notion of direction, which is to say, a straight line, always come to an end at some moment. More succinctly, the circular movements of the stars last indefinitely, but rectilinear movements have a finite duration. This opposition is confirmed by continual, empirical experience. So is it not an audacious paradox to claim that perfect motion, unaffected by exterior actions, lasting indefinitely, is a uniform rectilinear motion? What is evident is that this paradox is indispensable for defining the movements that are interesting to our terrestrial life. Nevertheless, Galileo could not have imagined a uniform rectilinear motion by moving rocks around a pasture or an armoire in a room, since these things come to a stop whenever one stops making an effort on them; he imagined it by lightly impelling a ball placed on a polished horizontal surface, and by choosing to neglect first the fact that the ball did come to a stop, and then the fact that it rolled and did not slide. As a result Galileo invented uniformly accelerated motion, and calculated its law by an integration, and, by letting a ball roll down various inclined planes, rediscovered something close to this law in the experiment and thus a relation between acceleration and the inclination of a plane. Gravity, defined up until then only in its relation with equilibrium, was thus found to be defined in its relation with the motion of falling bodies. The concept of force, a double concept, ambiguous, and a link between statics and dynamics, was thus invented; mass was distinguished from weight; dynamics was founded.

But the gropings were far from over. Motion apart from exterior actions was defined, and, in the same blow, friction appeared, the supposed cause of the running down of moving things left to themselves. A closed system had been defined: the one constituted by a constant force and a moving thing driven by this single force to the exclusion of all other action. The next step consisted in defining a set, exempt from exterior actions, of bodies in repose or in motion, subject or not to forces, acting on each other in a determined manner. To define such a set would be to find the means of embracing in a single effort of thought all its possible states, which consequently is to posit something identical and invariable through all its possible states. Thus Descartes, watching a game of billiards or bowls where the balls bumped each other on a horizontal plane, and thinking of a defined and closed system made up of elastic spheres, posited that the invariable was the quantity of motion, which is to say, the sum of the products of the masses multiplied by the speeds. The balls could not tell him whether he was right or wrong, for he was not thinking of them; these balls, after having rolled for a while over the green felt came to a stop, while Descartes thought of the balls as obeying the principle of inertia, perpetually in motion. But, as it turned out, his idea was not satisfactory. Later generations substituted for the product of the mass multiplied by the speed another product drawn from another study by the same Descartes.

Simple machines, such as the lever, pulley, winch, wedge, inclined plane, lessen the work of human beings, but not indefinitely; there remains, despite them, something undiminishable in human work. Descartes sought to define this irreducible something, and, at the same time, all simple machines. He assumed that the way a simple machine works is always analogous to the process of a man, who, taking on the job of lifting several weights to a certain height, lessens his fatigue by not lifting them all at once, but one at a time. Thus what is irreducible in the working of a simple machine will be the product of the weights multiplied by the distance that the heavy object traverses; this is a formula that agrees with that of the equilibrium of the lever that Archimedes discovered, and with that of acceleration on an inclined plane that Galileo discovered. Thus appeared the physical concept of work. After Descartes, we had the idea of relating this concept with motion. To all motion corresponds a possibility of work as defined by the mass and velocity of the moving object; this correspondence is established by the consideration of a ball that is rolling on a horizontal plane and then encounters an inclined plane; this ball rises to a height that is easy to calculate, and the product of this height multiplied by the weight of the ball is equal to half the product of the mass multiplied by the velocity squared, which is to say, to what we today call kinetic energy. The kinetic energy of a moving object at a given moment is therefore the work that would be accomplished by a ball of the same mass, moving on a horizontal plane with the same speed when it encountered an inclined plane. Or, what would come to the same thing, it is the work that gravity would accomplish on a body of the same mass that fell freely until it reached the same speed. A ball rolling on a horizontal plane theoretically has a constant speed; it therefore has also a constant kinetic energy. A falling body is presumed, in a first approximation, to be under a constant force; the space that it traverses, the speed, and the kinetic energy constantly vary; but as it falls from a set height, the sum of the space that it covers and the space that remains for it to cover, equal to this height, is constant, and consequently the sum of its kinetic energy and of the work that gravity can still accomplish on it is constant.

After giving up on trying to define closed mechanical systems by the quantity of motion, the attempt was made to define them by kinetic energy, or, what comes to the same thing, by sheer force, the double of kinetic energy; Huygens discovered that, if a number of bodies fell while being joined together, the sum of the forces is the same as if they had fallen separately. Several similar research efforts would lead to the principle of the conservation of force, the key to dynamics, according to which the force of a system depends on the forces that act on bodies and not on their interrelations. As one can always make a single resultant force correspond to several forces acting on a material point, all closed mechanical systems can be assimilated, with respect to force, to a material point moved by a single force. In the case of *no matter what* closed mechanical system, as in the case of a falling body, the sum of kinetic energy and of the work yet to be accomplished by the acting forces is a constant. Such is the principle of the conservation of energy. All such constructions deal with unchangeable bodies that are not susceptible to heating or cooling; but when one has finished the construction, one has to take account of the infinite difference, neglected up to this point, between these presumed movements and real movements that always do come to a stop. One takes account of it by something near to it—and this something is still an infinite error—thanks to the equivalence established between mechanical energy and other forms of energy, notably heat. The principle of the conservation of energy reaches its highest degree of generality. The formula is thus: "the sum of the mechanical equivalents of all actions that have been produced outside a system, when this passes in whatever manner, from a given state to a normal state, arbitrarily defined, is independent of the mode of passage."

[The ms. page ends at the previous sentence, having been torn off by Weil herself. This is the remainder after that. Ed.]

. . . the resistance of the air, for one who grabs a bucket of water on the ground, carries it one hundred meters, and puts it down again. On the contrary, by analogy with the elasticity of a weight, the fall of a weight is considered as work, work accomplished by gravity. If one is given a moving thing having a certain mass and traversing a certain distance, there will be work or not depending on whether or not the motion is uniform or accelerated. On the other hand, the kinetic energy of a moving thing at a given moment does not depend on its acceleration, but only on its velocity, thus although the concept of energy is defined by force and distance, a body that is moving by inertia has kinetic energy. The principle of inertia established a break between rest and uniform motion on one side, and all other movements on the other; on the contrary, the consideration of kinetic energy fixed the break between rest on one side, and the motion that it might be on the other, since all moving things of equal mass that have at an instant the same speed have at this instant the same kinetic energy, whatever the nature of their motion might be. But beyond that the concept of velocity is far from clear. The speed of a moving object at a given instant, though this might be a notion in current usage, has absolutely no significance except by its relation to the integral calculus; it is the derivative of the space traversed if this space is considered as a function of time. Thus for the word "velocity" to have a sense, it is necessary that the motion of the object be defined by a function, and a function that has a derivative for each value; said otherwise, it is necessary that the relation between the space traversed and time be identical to the relation between the coordinates of a curve having a tangent in each point. This means that it is the case for all bodies under a constant force, since the formula of the motion is that of a parabola; but a constant force means nothing except a constant acceleration, which is to say, a simple mathematical construction. Nothing indicates that real movements correspond to any function having any derivatives in all their parts nor, consequently, that something corresponds to kinetic energy.

NOTES

1. Weil uses this as an example in many places in her writings. The Greek understanding of numbers originally only encompassed what are called the rational numbers. These are whole numbers and fractions using whole numbers. Since they used lines and geometry to work numbers, rational numbers are represented by lines that are evenly divisible. They discovered, however, the irrational numbers, which, like the diagonal of a square, cannot be expressed as divisible in this way. The real numbers comprise a theory of numbers that incorporates both rational and irrational numbers, a resolution of the contradiction on a higher plane. (Ed.)

2. In several places in this essay when describing scientific results or experiments, Weil could have made things easier for her reader by using mathematical formulae. (She uses them herself in her notebooks.) However, as intimated here, she had an antipathy for algebraic formulae, and so appears to avoid them deliberately, preferring to give verbal explanations. (Ed.)

3. The original publication of this essay breaks off here. The remainder was originally published in French in *Sur la science* as a fragment, but it is now in the *Oeuvres complétes* as continuing the essay. (Ed.)

Index

ERIC O. SPRINGSTED

is the librarian at the Center of Theological Inquiry
and co-founder of the American Weil Society,
where he was its president for over thirty years.

Printed in the USA
CPSIA information can be obtained
at www.ICGtesting.com
CBHW051308181024
16057CB00006B/791